Connecting the Curriculum Through Interdisciplinary Instruction

JOHN H. LOUNSBURY, EDITOR

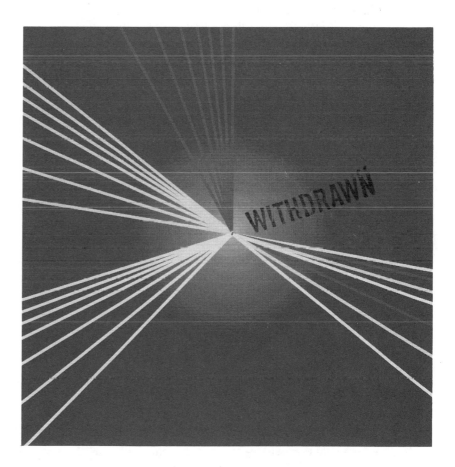

NATIONAL MIDDLE SCHOOL ASSOCIATION

NMSA

Most of the articles that comprise this volume appeared previously in the *Middle School Journal*. When appropriate, authors supplemented or updated their pieces. Some new articles and many additional features in the form of selected excerpts, quotes, lists, and charts have been included to increase the volume's usefulness.

Mary Mitchell, assistant to the editor, deserves special commendation for her careful work in formatting this volume for printing. Appreciation is also expressed to Robert Brindley, Christopher Reddick, and Abe Bonowitz for their photographs which enrich the publication and to Teri McCook for the cover design.

Copyright © 1992 by National Middle School Association
4151 Executive Parkway, Suite 300
Westerville, Ohio 43081
Fourth Printing, July 1999

ISBN: 1-56090-071-7

CONTENTS

T·E·A·M

TogetherEveryone Achieves More

Foreword

SUE SWAIM

The 1991-92 President of NMSA highlights the importance of interdisciplinary instruction and offers a challenge.

Education during the decade of the 90s will be noted for its intensified efforts to restructure curriculum, instruction, and assessment on pre-school through college levels. A significant part of this restructuring process has centered around the development and implementation of interdisciplinary teaming and interdisciplinary curricula. While this is by no means a new idea, the renewed enthusiasm for its potential to be a focal point for the development of a more relevant and meaningful curriculum for the learner cannot be ignored.

Certainly interdisciplinary education has been considered a key element of middle level education since the 1960s. Interdisciplinary teaching teams and multi-disciplinary and interdisciplinary units of study have been frequently found in middle level schools since the beginning of the movement. Flexible schedules, common planning time, staffing patterns, and school buildings have all been created or changed to support interdisciplinary education. Yet, despite all these efforts the actual implementation of interdisciplinary education continues to fall short of its full potential. While we've come to realize the importance of living in an interdisciplinary world and the need for schools to reflect this reality, it has remained difficult to restructure our pigeon-holed, content-separated curriculum to a more interdisciplinary/integrated one.

The challenge which faces middle level educators today is to expand our vision and our implementation of interdisciplinary education. Even where interdisciplinary teaching teams and units of study exist they often stop short of actually restructuring curriculum, instruction, and assessment. Completing three or four interdisciplinary units of study per year should be viewed as part of the transition to an interdisciplinary curriculum … not as THE interdisciplinary curriculum.

I am confident this book will be a valuable resource for middle level educators striving to implement interdisciplinary education. Its true value will be measured by how readers use the ideas and strategies presented here to push the status quo beyond current expectations and install truly integrated education. Together we must continue to stretch the vision and challenge old assumptions about what we teach and how we teach so the goal of a meaningful and relevant curriculum based upon the needs and characteristics of young adolescent learners can be achieved. ▲

Interdisciplinary Team Organization Supported by 1988 National Middle School Association Resolution

Whereas, when middle school teachers share a common group of students and have quality time to discuss the special needs, interests, and styles of those students, miracles can occur, and *Whereas,* in middle schools, the interdisciplinary team is the organizational unit that facilitates this collaborative planning and teaching, and *Whereas,* as middle schools continue to increase in size and complexity, the interdisciplinary team promotes a climate of smallness essential to student success and teacher efficacy, and *Whereas,* departmentalization does not enable teachers from varying subject areas to collaborate regularly nor does it promote the quality of teacher-student involvement essential to the effective middle school,

Therefore, be it resolved that middle school personnel affirm the interdisciplinary team organization as the most appropriate arrangement for middle level teachers and students.

Interdisciplinary Instruction: A Mandate for the Nineties

JOHN H. LOUNSBURY

Connecting the curriculum via interdisciplinary instruction is not an optional activity for middle level educators — it's mandatory.

The junior high school is not meeting the needs of its students. Such a view had come to be generally accepted by the 1960s. And to alter that reality in rode the middle school with promises of reform. The subject-centered and compartmentalized junior high school day, a carbon copy of the high school, was the major concern. To counter it, middle school advocates offered interdisciplinary teaming in which several subject area teachers would be responsible for a common group of students and collaborate on instruction.

Almost immediately the concept of teaming became the key characteristic of the new middle school. It has come to be seen as the *sine qua non* of a real middle school. Probably no single word has been more frequently cited in relationship to the middle school than has the word *interdisciplinary*. As the movement has grown the resolve to counter the fragmentation of the typical subject-centered day has become even firmer. And teaming continues as the major means advanced to connect the curriculum. Its importance as an educational practice simply cannot be ignored.

Teaching in a middle level school during this last decade of the twentieth century will inevitably require one to give serious consideration to the benefits of interdisciplinary instruction and take some action in relationship to it. The push to integrate instruction is strong and will not abate. Even those middle level schools that for one reason or another choose not to establish teams will still have to confront the issue. This is not a matter that can simply be waited out.

The integration of separate subject instruction is not just another "innovation" that will fade away in due time. Successful middle school teachers in the year 2000 will be those who have been able to rise up out of their certification comfort zones and see themselves as much more than single subject instructors. There simply will be no place for those unable to redefine and broaden their roles in the effective middle school of the next century. Not only will all middle level schools become involved in efforts to unify learning and connect the curriculum, but high schools in substantial numbers will take up the torch of interdisciplinary instruction, as a small but surprising number already have. Increasingly it is being recognized that there will be no significant "restructuring" of schools until reform efforts attack and make fundamental changes in the curriculum of content and the instructional approaches utilized — what and how kids learn.

If such be the case, as I firmly believe it is, then it behooves all who are involved in the education of 10-14 year olds to become thoroughly grounded in the theory and practice of interdisciplinary instruction. There is much to teaming; it is complex and evolves slowly; it calls for adjustments and compromises. Evaluation procedures must undergo revision, and the need for varied instructional materials increases greatly.The creation of interdisciplinary teams with common planning time and a block schedule is a prerequisite for interdisciplinary instruction. However, administratively organizing teams only provides opportunities. It is a great mistake to establish teams and declare victory.

It is especially important to recognize that implementing interdisciplinary instruction will require a change in the teacher's role. Unless the teachers themselves are willing and able to alter some established practices, the gains from placing them on a team will be minimal. As Henry David Thoreau wisely warned us, "Beware of enterprises that require new clothes and not rather a new wearer of clothes."

Because of the new demands and changes in established routines that entering into teaming requires, few teams reach their potential during the first two or three years — some never do. Although conducting real interdisciplinary instruction is not an early expectation of teaming it should remain as a stated goal to be sought by all. The materials in this volume will give guidance to both beginners in teaming and those in established teams who are now ready for actually initiating integrated instruction built around the solving of problems rather than simply relating instruction in several subjects. Some articles describe well-developed correlation approaches, others illustrate bolder ventures that involve a whole grade in a project.

Creating interdisciplinary teams in every school serving 10-14 year olds would be a giant step forward. Significant benefits to youth would result as teachers collaborate on various routines and occasionally correlate their presentations, even fusing subjects once in awhile. The administratively-mandated twice-a-year thematic unit, however, does not justify business as usual (read: departmentalized instruction) the rest of the time. Unfortunately, the experiences of the last two decades have shown that changes in the content of schooling do not automatically follow from organizing teams.

Interdisciplinary instruction, even when done rather comprehensively, is not a panacea. Teachers, while eagerly moving to connect the curriculum through interdisciplinary instruction need to understand that teaming has its weaknesses and its limitations. These are addressed in the closing article. ▲

The individual child must be the focus of all
instruction, no matter how it is carried out.

THE STATUS OF TEAMING

Selected data from *Education in the Middle Grades: National Practices and Trends,* by Joyce L. Epstein and Douglas J. Mac Iver. National Middle School Association, 1990.

- About 42% of early adolescent students receive instruction from interdisciplinary teams of teachers somewhere between grades 5 and 9.

- The bottom line is that at this time most schools do not use interdisciplinary teams, including about 60% of the middle schools and 75% of other grade organizations. Most students in the middle grades (58%) do not receive instruction from interdisciplinary teams.

- About 40% of the teams have no leader to coordinate and organize team activities. According to principals, teams with leaders spend more time on team activities and attain more benefits from teaming.

- About 30% of the schools that organize teams provide no common planning time for the teachers to meet together. Just over one-third of the schools that use teams give teachers two or more hours of common planning time.

- Teachers spend almost half of their common planning time on individual work, not on team work.

- The researchers concluded: "If teaming is to be the keystone of middle grades education, schools have a long way to go to develop effective interdisciplinary teams of teachers."

SECTION I

What Interdisciplinary Instruction Can Do for You

Erb   **Thomas O. Erb,** Associate Professor of Education,
University of Kansas, Lawrence, KS

Arhar   **Joanne Arhar,** Assistant Professor of Education,
University of South Florida, Tampa, FL

Johnston   **J. Howard Johnston,** Professor and Chair, Department of
Secondary Education, University of South Florida, Tampa, FL

Markle   **Glenn C. Markle,** Professor of Education, University
of Cincinnati, Cincinnati, OH

Davies   **Mary A. Davies,** Assistant Professor, Department of
Teacher Education, Southern Utah University, Cedar City, UT

What Team Organization Can Do for Teachers

THOMAS O. ERB

Two hundred teachers who were organized into teams described the many positive aspects of this organizational scheme.

For several years the interdisciplinary team has been touted in the middle school literature as the preferred way to organize basic subject teachers. The team has been extolled as the best way to bridge the gap for students between self-contained arrangements of elementary schools and the departmentalized classrooms of secondary schools. Students are supposed to benefit from greater academic support and enjoy the virtues of an integrated curriculum. Dealt with much less often is the issue of what team organization can do for the teachers who implement it. However, the growing concern about the professional worklife of teachers makes this a good time to examine team organization from the teachers' perspective.

The interdisciplinary team is a powerful organizational arrangement that is improving the professional worklife of many middle grades teachers. Little (1982) found that in successful schools, more than in unsuccessful ones, teachers participated in the norms of collegiality as they pursued greater range of professional interactions with fellow teachers and administrators. Teachers in teams not only demonstrated frequent discussion with colleagues about instruction, student progress, and curriculum but also tended to play active roles in building-level decision-making.

Goodman (1979) showed how organizational innovation had a dual focus to improve productivity and bring positive psychological outcomes. Ashton and Webb (1986) documented how team organization in the middle grades can improve educational productivity in the form of increased student achievement. The psychological outcomes for teachers, administrators, and support personnel can also provide us with a model for analyzing the impact of interdisciplinary teams on the overall organization of schools and the rewards that teachers perceive.

Goodman contended that successful organizational changes required the simultaneous restructuring of multiple aspects of the organization. He identified four aspects that need to be restructured: the authority system, the decision-making system, the reward system, and the communication system. The purpose of reorganization was "to provide greater democratization of the workplace, greater control for the worker over his or her environment and greater joint problem-solving between labor and management." Team organization, which is currently in place in many middle grades schools, is an effective way to accomplish these purposes.

7

Team organization is a more fundamental structural change than the team teaching that was popular in the 1960s and early 1970s. There are four organizational aspects that define team organization. Two of these aspects are absolutely essential. Without them interdisciplinary teams do not exist. These two essential elements are (1) common planning time or team meeting time and (2) shared students. All teachers on the team share the same students and are collectively responsible for their basic instruction. Two additional conditions facilitate the full functioning of interdisciplinary teams but are not absolutely essential for their success. These are a common block-of-time teaching schedule and common team space composed of adjacent classrooms and the connecting hallways.

Recently nearly two-hundred teachers who were organized into teams were interviewed along with their administrators and support staff such as counselors and librarians. Interdisciplinary teams in all schools visited included basic subject teachers (English, math, social studies, and science). Many schools also involved exploratory and elective teachers such as art, music, physical education, home economics, and industrial arts teachers on interdisciplinary teams. All interviewed teachers served in one of twelve 6-8 or 7-8 schools ranging in size from 300 to 1000 students. Some of these schools were in their first year of team organization, others had been doing it for 16 years, while most were in their fifth or sixth year of team organization.

What emerged from these interviews was a pattern of effective staff deployment. Interdisciplinary team organization showed how each of Goodman's (1979) systems worked together to reinforce a positive work environment for teachers and administrators alike.

Authority System

The authority system refers to *who* makes decisions and *what* types of decisions are made. The next section on the decision-making system will focus on *how* decisions are made. In middle grades schools with team organization, teachers engaged in joint decision-making on several issues. Team members generally decided, as a group, rules of conduct and expectations for students. Teams generally had group input into retention decisions that were made near the end of each school year. Long before detention decisions were made, team teachers would discuss students and make joint decisions on how best to support a student who had begun to "fall through the cracks." Teachers seemed confident of their decisions about students, because as one teacher put it, "We all see problems, not just a personality." This teacher was referring to the fact that because of mutual discussion of students' progress, teachers were better able to

The team is a powerful organizational arrangement that improves the worklife of middle grades teachers.

Two essential elements are: (1) common planning time, and (2) shared students.

isolate and diagnose problems and not just react to students' personalities. Several principals and counselors emphasized to me how well they thought teachers kept on top of students' problems and made decisions to act together to help these students.

Access occurred in one of two ways. In some cases principals met regularly with team leaders who carried the ideas and concerns of teachers to the principals. In several other schools the principals scheduled themselves into team meetings on a regular basis, sometimes as often as once a week. In both cases teachers had the opportunity to discuss issues and concerns and have their input conveyed either directly or indirectly to the principal. One principal stated that teams were better for dealing with administrative problems than the official Educational Advisory Council.

Team meetings are a vital crucible for generating ideas for improving schools. The time for teachers to talk with colleagues and support staff generates ideas that lead to improving the working of schools. This process does not occur nearly as often in schools where teachers are isolated in self-contained or departmental classrooms. Teachers on teams are involved in a broader range of decisions affecting a greater range of school-wide issues than are teachers in other settings where decision-making is more often limited to their own classrooms. In schools with team organization, teachers are more likely to have input into decisions on school-wide discipline rules, grade card design, scheduling, student orientation procedures, class size, assembly schedules, and the design and use of forms that are used in administering the building.

In addition to having greater input on school-wide issues, teachers on teams also make decisions on a team wide basis on such issues as adopting team goals, developing discipline rules, adopting team mascots and themes, designing systems for rewarding students, and several other issues that are bigger than a single classroom. One particularly important area for teacher decision-making on a team concerns the placement and grouping of students. Teachers can group and regroup students within a team for academic or behavioral reasons in a way departmentalized teachers cannot do without upsetting the master schedule. Teachers organized into interdisciplinary teams are involved in a greater range of decisions beyond the boundaries of their own classrooms than are teachers in less facilitative organizations.

Two additional conditions facilitate the full functioning of teams: (1) a common block-of-time, and (2) common team space in adjacent classrooms and connecting hallways.

Teachers on teams are involved in a broader range of decisions affecting a greater range of school-wide issues than are teachers in other settings.

Decision-making System

The way decisions are made in schools with interdisciplinary teams varies from the way decisions are typically made in schools organized in other ways. Two types of decisions need to be considered. First, teacher input into school-wide decisions will be examined by using an example from a school with five teams: three grade-level basic subject teams; one related arts team; and one support team consisting of school librarian, counselor, psychologist, nurse, and special educators.

In this school no decisions on school-wide issues were ever made at faculty meetings that had not already been discussed in the team meetings by groups of four to six faculty members. The identification of school problems needing attention would take place in one of the team meetings. For example, the eighth grade team members were dissatisfied with the alternate schedule used on assembly days because it penalized some classes and teachers unfairly. So the teachers on this team devised a new assembly day schedule.

They then presented their plan to the principal who put it on the agenda of the school-wide faculty meeting. The principal presented the proposal to the total faculty and told them to discuss it in their team meetings so that it could be acted on at the next faculty meeting. In this school nothing came up for a faculty vote that teachers did not have an opportunity to discuss thoroughly in small groups. Indeed, most of the ideas for improvement were originally generated by faculty members meeting together in team meetings.

Teachers also had much input into decisions that more directly affected their teaching. Teachers on teams worked together to solve problems. If a student was having difficulty in one teacher's class, that teacher could discuss the problem with several colleagues. This led to joint decision-making by team members to devise a plan to help that student through a troubling time. When two, three, or four teachers reached a joint decision to help a student, they mutually reinforced each other in working with that student.

Sometimes a problem appeared to be beyond the immediate resources available on the team. The team then would decide to invite the counselor to the team meeting for advice on how to proceed with the student. The counselor might supply the team members with background information on a student and help them decide on a course of action that might directly involve the counselor or even lead to a parent conference. In any case, the teamed teachers made decisions about the nature of the problem and about the course of action to be followed.

> **No decisions on school-wide issues were ever made at faculty meetings that had not already been discussed in team meetings.**

Focussing on team decision-making illustrates why team planning time and shared students are such important factors in characterizing interdisciplinary team organization. The team meetings provide the time that is essential for teachers to talk out concerns and ideas that they have. Since the most central aspect of teaching is instructing young people, the fact that many students are shared by several teachers (each of whom sees these students in a slightly different context) allows teachers the opportunity to pool their perspectives on each student to develop a more complete picture of how that student is doing in school.

Reward System

The psychological rewards of team organization for teachers were repeated in building after building by first-year teachers and sixteen-year veterans alike. Teachers who have never teamed often worried about whether they would get along with all their team members and about whether they would be able to "be themselves" in their classrooms. By contrast teachers who have experienced team organization reported that their own classroom teaching was enriched and that they greatly appreciated the camaraderie of their colleagues.

The word *support* kept coming up over and over again. Sometimes teachers were talking about support in parent-teacher conferences where a particularly difficult student was being discussed. Sometimes teachers talked about the support they received from teammates on classroom management issues. New teachers talked about the support they felt in working with people who developed relationships with them and with whom they were able to talk about kids. The fact that their students knew that a new teacher had a special relationship with other teachers was perceived by new teachers to be supportive.

As team members, these teachers felt less isolated. Even some veteran teachers reported having difficult years when team membership provided the moral support that carried them through the year. One teacher indicated that she had just experienced her worst year in fifteen years of teaching. However, the regular team meetings with adults helped her work through her problems with the kids in her classroom. Some teachers even talked about their teams as providing the support of group therapy. As one teacher put it, "Before team organization came along we were starving for adult attention."

While getting to know colleagues better and developing "a tremendous feeling of belonging" are powerful psychological rewards for team members, teachers on teams have the opportunity to

> **Team meetings provide the time that is essential for teachers to talk through concerns and ideas.**

> **Teachers who have experienced team organization reported their teaching was enriched and the camaraderie of their colleagues was appreciated.**

expand their roles as teachers without leaving the classroom. The previous sections on authority and decision-making indicate how the teacher roles are expanding in building governance. Teachers see themselves as having more input into the decisions that affect their work lives. In addition, team membership provides new opportunities for leadership. These opportunities come not only from organizing and conducting team meetings, but also from communicating team actions to outsiders and from the growth potential of presenting oneself before one's peers.

As to whether one must sacrifice one's unique teaching style to be an effective team member, the answer appears to be "no." Instead it appears that team organization actually enriches variety rather than suppresses it. One teacher put it this way, "We teach different types of classes, but they are each better."

While sometimes a teacher is placed on a team into which he does not fit, and while it is true that teachers need to cooperate in order to be good team members, team organization is proving to be a more rewarding arrangement for the vast majority of teachers who are involved in it than were the alternative arrangements that teachers had previously experienced. A former departmentalized eighth-grade English teacher in Kansas now in her second year of teaming said. "If they do away with teaming, I'll quit teaching!" An eighteen-year veteran with five years' experience as a team member related, "The middle school team is the best thing I've ever seen in teaching."

Communication System

The fourth of Goodman's (1979) mutually reinforcing components of organizational change was the communication system. One of the most powerful aspects of interdisciplinary team organizational change is the communication it fosters among teachers.

Communication among teachers on a team is greatly improved. Several teachers and administrators pointed out that they felt the biggest difference between departmentalized schools and teamed schools was the talk among teachers about students. Students in schools with team organization were talked about much more often by teachers and in greater depth than were students elsewhere. Teachers on teams communicated about specific students and devised ways to support those students. Teachers on teams also talked more about curriculum. English teachers knew what math and science teachers were doing and vice versa. Field trips were often planned jointly by team members to coordinate with several subjects being taught on the team. Joint units were often planned to coordinate English and

As one teacher put it, "Before team organization came along we were starving for adult attention."

"If they do away with teaming, I'll quit teaching!"
— A former departmentalized teacher

science or social studies and English. A third area in which teachers communicated on a team related to administrative or managerial issues. These included such things as seeking discipline expectations.

Yet another area that teachers communicated about on a team was staff development. Team meetings were frequently devoted to issues about which the teachers wished to gain new skills. At least two schools used the team meeting time to improve teachers' conferencing skills prior to the implementation of new parent conferencing programs. Team organization changed the ways teachers communicated with each other.

Team organization also altered the frequency and substance of communications between teachers and other actors in the educational drama. Communication with parents was reported to be more frequent when teams existed than when teachers were isolated in departmentalized classrooms. Not only were more face-to-face conferences held (often during team meeting time), but more phone conversations took place. Contacts with the home usually occurred earlier in the development of a problem than they did in other school organizations. Through their own communications about students, teachers identified those problems sooner. In schools with team organization, parents were more likely to receive letters and newsletters that kept them informed.

Communication with school counselors was both increased and altered by team organization. As mentioned before, counselors often provided background information on a student being discussed in a team meeting. Counselors kept team members informed of follow-up activity concerning students. Several counselors commented on how much easier it was to reach teamed teachers because these teachers were all in one place during team planning time. On the other hand, counselors reported that they were someone teachers could go to with a group problem needing team attention. Many counselors felt that their services were better used in schools with team organization, in large part because of the improved communication with teachers.

Earlier in discussing authority and decision-making, communication between teachers and principals was examined. Principals felt that they had greater access to teacher expertise. The ease of gaining access to teacher opinion in team meetings greatly increased teacher-administrator dialogue on a whole range of issues affecting the governing of a school.

A fourth category of outside persons with whom team teachers communicated was a team coordinator. This person might be an assistant principal, a counselor, or a teacher who acted as a coordina-

Communication with parents was more frequent when teams existed than when teachers were isolated in departmentalized classrooms.

> **The frequency of face-to-face dialogue added to the sophistication of teacher communication and reduced paper work.**

tor to foster cross-team communication. This person typically meets with team leaders or with whole teams regularly and serves as a communications link across teams to coordinate such issues as curriculum, testing, and materials allocation.

The greater frequency of face-to-face dialogue that was fostered in team settings not only added to the sophistication of teacher communication, but it often cut down on paper work, that eternal bane of the teaching profession. In one school regular face-to-face meetings with the special education staff eliminated the need for a reporting form that had been used previously in a departmentalized setting to exchange information on how well special students were doing. Other teams have found that joint progress reports and joint eligibility reports cut paper work and increase the richness of teacher communication.

Conclusions

Team organization has long been promoted in the middle grades as a way to bridge the gap for students between the self-contained elementary arrangement, and the completely departmentalized secondary classrooms. In addition to the advantage for students, team organization offers a promising way to deploy teachers more effectively. The team meeting is the key to altering the ways teachers relate to each other and to educators and parents. The domains over which teachers make decisions are expanded. They also have greater input into building-wide administrative decisions. Not only do teachers have input into more types of decisions, but the quality of their involvement in decision-making is improved by having the time built into their workdays for team meetings. Teachers, nearly universally, report greater satisfaction with the conditions of teaching when they are organized into interdisciplinary teams. In the current drive to upgrade the teaching profession, serious attention needs to be given to establishing more interdisciplinary teams in the middle grades. Both students and teachers would find junior highs and middle schools more rewarding places to be . ▲

REFERENCES

Ashton, P.T., & Webb, R.B. (1986). *Making a difference: Teachers' sense of efficacy and student achievement.* New York: Longman Inc.

Goodman, P.S. (1979). *Assessing organizational change: The Rushton quality of work experiment.* New York: Wiley & Sons.

Little, J.W. (1982). Norms of collegiality and experimentation: Workplace conditions of school success. *American Educational Research Journal, 19.* 325-340.

An individual can make a difference — a team can make a miracle.
— Sierra Middle School, Tucson, AZ

The Effects of Teaming and Collaborative Arrangements

JOANNE M. ARHAR, J. HOWARD JOHNSTON, GLENN C. MARKLE

Research in this area is still in its infancy, but several positive results of teaming are already clearly apparent.

For a long time, middle level teachers have not been perceived as a distinct professional group by the institutions that prepare them, the states that certify them, or the researchers that study them. As a result, the effect of any school practice, organizational or otherwise, on the teachers in the middle level institution has not been adequately studied. Therefore, middle school research linked to teacher outcomes is very limited. Middle school research on the teacher outcomes associated with interdisciplinary teaming is in its infancy.

Chissom et al. (1986) explored several factors strongly associated with professional satisfaction in middle schools. The results of their questionnaire, consisting of two open-ended questions regarding factors which encouraged and discouraged teachers to perform their best, revealed that faculty cooperation was the highest rated encouraging category. Cooperation consisted of elements such as cooperation among teachers, influence of teachers, interaction with colleagues, utilization of team concepts, supportive administration, positive feedback from supervisors, and outstanding faculty colleagues. This study focused on the workplace conditions associated with teacher efficacy and the presence of conditions, such as teaming, that promoted coopera-

tion among teachers that were shown to be essential for teacher satisfaction.

In an examination of the characteristics of effective inner-city intermediate schools, Levine (et al., 1984) described academically successful schools in Watts, Brooklyn, the Bronx, and Detroit. Organizational arrangements which created a more personal, caring environment for teachers and students were considered important innovations related to school improvement. Team organization which fostered team planning and students' personal growth was considered essential to the improvement process. Teams of teachers working with small groups of students can reduce isolation, anonymity, and alienation from the institution and, evidently, not only increase teacher satisfaction but be a significant factor in success with high-risk populations as well.

A study designed to gather evidence about the effectiveness of contemporary middle school education in the United States (George & Oldaker, 1985) revealed that the interdisciplinary team contributed greatly to staff morale. "Previously isolated instructors became team members and developed the same sense of belonging and camaraderie they hoped to instill in their students. The flexibility in scheduling inherent to team responsibility for a common group of students occupying generally the same area provided teachers with many options for instruction. Sharing knowledge of students and subjects increased their confidence and consistency" (p. 28).

It appears then that the use of an interdisciplinary team arrangement does have the potential for influencing instruction. And, while the details of this opportunity for instructional diversity and its effects on student learning are elusive, the potential for its presence in team arrangements is a fruitful area for further study.

Once exposed to teaming, teachers are quick to advocate its benefits. Blomquist et al. (1986) investigated the relationship between job satisfaction/morale and organizational changes in a junior high school. Among the factors they examined was interdisciplinary teaming and its affect on a variety of outcomes including morale and collegial communication. Teachers reported satisfaction generated by teaming and collegial communication. They said they liked to be a part of a teaching team and they preferred working on a team to working individually. Another teacher felt that teaming positively affected working conditions because it allows for a better "hold" on students.

This study also uncovered one of the concerns associated with teaming. Specialist teachers (music, P. E., foreign language, etc.) wished out loud that they could be members of teams as well. She believed that such an arrangement would facilitate conversations about students. However, it seems as if the concern may be rooted even more deeply in some settings. In another study (Johnston, 1987) non-team teachers reported a sense of isolation stemming from not being on a teaching team. Further, in some schools, these feelings were elevated to outright anger and the belief that, as one specialist put it, "the teams ran the schools; we are the tail being wagged by the team dog."

From the responses on the communication section of the Blomquist study (1986), it appears that teams do little beyond discussing individual students at weekly team meetings. The majority of the staff felt that they did not have time to share ideas and materials with colleagues. They also found that staff with low levels of emotional exhaustion have time to communicate with colleagues whereas those with high levels of emotional exhaustion do not. Staff with low levels of depersonalization (callousness, cynicism, and insensitivity toward students) also felt they have time to talk with colleagues while staff with high levels of depersonalization do not feel they have time to talk to colleagues. The researchers do not offer an explanation of these results, but the results seem to suggest a set of prior personal

Teams working with small groups can reduce isolation, anonymity and alienation, and be a significant factor in success with high-risk populations.

Teachers reported they liked to be a part of a team and preferred working on a team to working individually.

conditions which influence teachers to interact with each other that may have absolutely nothing to do with organizational arrangements. In this sense, it is a chicken-egg question: do people exhibit low levels of depersonalization and emotional exhaustion because they are team members, or are they successful team members because they have low levels of emotional exhaustion and depersonalization? At present, the results are inconclusive.

In this study (Blomquist, 1986), the researchers also speculated that job satisfaction may have been related to the clarity with which the teachers understood the goals of teacher teaming and grouping of students. Evidently, it is also essential that such clarity be accompanied by an awareness of the rewards that are in the teaming arrangement for them (Johnston, 1987).

Non-team teachers reported a sense of isolation. In some schools, these feelings were elevated to outright anger.

In Lipsitz's (1982) account of successful schools for young adolescents, interdisciplinary teaming is a common element in each of the four schools identified as exemplary. According to Lipsitz, staff organization permits cooperative work, but does not require it. The level of interdependence among teachers on teams varies from school to school. In some schools, team teachers meet only to solve student scheduling and placement problems, not to work out matters of curricular and instructional importance.

Despite the prevalence of teaming in Lipsitz's study, though, in only one school do teachers identify the team structure as the most representative feature of their school. Noe Middle School is an open-plan school for 1000 sixth, seventh and eighth graders. Each of the seven academic teams shares the responsibility for the learning experiences of 150 students. With the encouragement and guidance of the principal and team leaders, teachers use school resources and team planning time to make autonomous decisions regarding grouping, departmentalization, interdisciplinary units, allocation of time, intramurals, teacher-based guidance, and team rules. The primary focus is on working together to best deal with each child as an individual.

Collegial interaction about students and scheduling predominate. Teachers tend to use the team structure for less difficult tasks.

Lipsitz claims that "Teaching performance is not a function of personal qualities alone. It results from the joint efforts and sanctions of highly motivated and competitive groups" (p. 98). There is some evidence that teachers learn from each other because of visibility afforded by open space. "A student teacher comments that she need only look around her in the team area to be exposed to several different instructional methods" (p. 118) . However, Lipsitz also adds that teaching styles tend to be more alike on teams. Since the team selection process is not described, the uniformity may have to do with teacher self-selection into the most familiar, comfortable, teaching situation. Uniformity, however, is not the ideal consequence of team instruction. There is no evidence reported to suggest that teachers systematically observe each other teaching and provide feedback.

Finally, in this study teachers characterized themselves as professionals because of their decision-making power. "They discuss ideas together, reach group consensus, and have the support of the team for the humdrum and the adventuresome in the school day. Teaching is not a lonely profession'' (p. 99). Clearly, it is the opportunity to engage in this type of exchange that empowers teachers. Whether they elect to avail themselves fully of this opportunity or not, the power to do so is in their hands.

The team structure appears to have achieved some degree of task and reward interdependence associated with the requirements for a cooperative structure. Collegial interaction about students and scheduling predominate, supporting earlier research that teachers tend to use the team structure for less difficult tasks.

The opportunity to engage in decision-making empowers teachers.

The notable departure from the cohesiveness of the academic teams at Noe Middle School (and in others described by Johnston, 1987) is the fragmentation of the unified arts team which lacks a common group of students and a common planning time. The result appears to be a lack of interest in producing a coordinated curriculum and a measure of "bickering" among the teachers about students.

In a 1984 pilot study of middle level collegial teaming, Little and Bird studied the organization and maintenance of a policy of teaming in an urban middle school with an ethnically diverse enrollment of 850 students. An interdisciplinary curriculum provided a common focus for different levels of teams who received strong support from the principal. Joint action among teachers appears to depend on the teachers' perception of their interdependence and the presence of opportunities for joint action.

Three situations interfered with their operating procedures providing evidence that teachers are more likely to work together when they feel their problems can be better solved through the efforts of a group who share the problem and when bureaucratic conditions (schedules, staff assignments, and resources) and cultural conditions (beliefs, norms which encourage or discourage teaming) are reduced.

Interdependence and opportunity governed teacher responses and actions in three situations involving an influx of student teachers, turnover among members of established teams, and the appointment of a new school principal less committed to the team approach.

The study suggested that three kinds of joint action can be identified: coordinated activity, conducted individually but similarly; accommodating activity, involving individual adjustment to meet the needs of others; and cooperative activity, the mutual, face-to-face interaction of teachers to achieve a joint goal.

Several studies have been designed to compare middle level and junior high organizational structures. Bryan and Erickson (1970) studied teacher perceptions and opinions in a middle school with an interdisciplinary team organization and a junior high school with a departmental structure. They examined, among other things, teachers' attitudes about and perception of their relationships with colleagues, administrators, and students.

From their questionnaire data, they found few significant differences between the two groups of teachers. Teachers did differ in attitude toward students. Middle level teachers tended to characterize the academic competence and promise of their students while junior high teachers tended to describe students in terms of academic and disciplinary deficiencies. In terms of teacher satisfaction, they found that middle school teachers were slightly more satisfied with school than their junior high counterparts.

> **Middle school teachers were slightly more satisfied with school than their junior high counterparts.**

As a part of their study of the relationship between teachers' sense of efficacy and student achievement, Ashton and Webb (1986) studied two organizationally different schools for sixth, seventh and eight graders — a traditional junior high school with a departmental organization, single-age grouping, and homeroom, and a middle school organized around interdisciplinary teams, multi-age grouping and an advisory program — to understand how school organization influences teacher thought and behavior. Schools were similar in enrollment and student body composition.

Although the primary focus of their work was not collaboration, their case studies do serve to illustrate the differences in teacher attitudes, beliefs, and practices associated with collaborative and noncollaborative organizational structures. The theoretical orientation of their work led them to hypothesize that school organization that encourages collegial interaction among teachers may enhance teacher efficacy by creating an atmosphere of support.

> **Organizational differences promote different relationships among teachers and different views of teaching.**

Results indicated that organizational differences in the two schools promoted quite different relationships among teachers and different views of teaching. The teams produced a sense of community and shared commitment which diminished teacher isolation and uncertainty about effectiveness. Shared responsibility for a group of students, shared decisions governing classroom practice, shared

19

planning time, planning space, and proximity of classrooms gave teachers a sense of common focus, common sense of accomplishment, and source of emotional and professional support in solving problems.

The net result was the forging of strong, collegial relationships. Friendships were also initiated and maintained by the team organization. These friendships ultimately helped to maintain the smooth functioning of the team. Teachers admitted, however, that collaborative work was demanding because working out joint decisions took a great deal of energy.

Teachers admitted that collaborative work was demanding.

Conflict with colleagues was sometimes viewed as a problem. Finally, although teaching was carried out by individuals in individual classrooms, teachers in interdisciplinary teams viewed teaching as a communal rather than individual enterprise. Whether or not this involved teachers actually observing each other teach, providing feedback or evaluation is not indicated.

Collegial relationships and teacher views of teaching differed markedly at the non-teamed school. Departmentalization was not intended to be a highly interactive decision-making structure. Interdependence was not encouraged by the department or committees. Teachers usually divided up work and met only to report on their individual solutions. "Teachers saw themselves as individual members of the staff doing separate jobs with relative independence . . . They shared few responsibilities with other teachers nor did they want to, for they valued their relative autonomy. Their successes were their own and others learned of their problems only to the degree that teachers themselves wished to reveal them" (p. 115).

Teachers looked to each other to solve problems and were rewarded by the support of colleagues.

Decisions governing school life were made by the administration, occasionally with input from the staff. Friendships may have been initiated at school but were maintained outside of the school. Less conflict between teachers was reported. And finally, teaching was defined as an individual skill and a good school as a well-organized collection of talented teachers doing their work independently and well.

It appears then that the joint focus inherent in the team structure resulted in greater task and reward interdependence in team teachers. Teachers looked to each other to solve problems and were rewarded by the support and approval of their colleagues. Increased collegial conflicts seemed to result from a joint decision-making process, but they seemed to be accepted by the team members as a necessary part of the organizational arrangement.

Teams diminished isolation and uncertainty. The lack of such a joint focus in the departmental structure offered little opportunity for task and reward interdependence. As indicated in earlier studies, there is no evidence provided that in either school teachers actually collaborated, specifically and purposefully, on the improvement of curriculum or teaching practice.

Teamed teachers moved in and out of each other's classrooms, but data do not suggest they actually made formal observations. The opportunity did, however, apparently exist.

The authors concluded that teaching teams, adviser-advisee programs, multiaged grouping, and clear and shared educational aims appeared to lessen teachers' self-doubts and to diminish the self-protective, low-efficacy ideologies that accompany such doubts. The complexity of the organizational structure appeared to lead to increased interdependence among teachers which supports earlier research that task complexity leads to greater interdependence.

The authors of this study caution readers not to judge one school as more effective than the other. Nor do they claim that one method of organization promotes collaborative practices whereas the other does not. They recognize that some schools without teams are very collaborative while others with teams are lacking in collaborative practices.

The conclusions that can be drawn from this review are tentative but promising. It is clear that team arrangements reduce teacher isolation, increase satisfaction, and improve individual teachers' sense of efficacy. Teaming is also more likely to promote discussions of individual student needs and the operational details of teaching, a finding that parallels very closely George's (1984) description of the early stages of development teams go through.

As might be expected, though, a single organizational arrangement does not assure that collaboration will occur on such important matters as instructional improvement or curricular integration. Often, the team is viewed not as an entity, but as a collection of individuals with different expertise who defer to one another on matters related closely to that expertise (i.e., curriculum and instruction in a given subject).

At the same time, the shared decision-making opportunities present on a team seem to enhance the teachers' sense of power and control, and increase the likelihood that they will engage in cooperative endeavors. So, while it appears that teaming arrangements are not

Team arrangements reduce teacher isolation, increase satisfaction, and improve individual teachers' sense of efficacy.

Teaming arrangements are not sufficient to cause collaboration; they are only a prerequisite for such cooperation.

sufficient to cause collaboration, they are a necessary prerequisite for such cooperation among teachers. ▲

References

Ashton, P.T. & Webb, R.B. (1986). *Making a difference: Teacher's sense of efficacy and student achievement.* New York: Longman, Inc.

Blomquist, R., Bornstein, S., Fink, G., Michaud, R., Oja, S.N. & Smulyan, L. (1986). Action research on change in schools: The relationship between teacher moral/job satisfaction and organizational changes in a junior high school. (Report no. 81-0040). Washington D.C.: National Institute of Education.

Bryan, C., & Erickson, E. (1970). *Structural effects on school behavior: A comparison of middle school and junior high school programs.* Grand Rapids, MI: Grand Rapids Public Schools. ED 064-754.

Chissom, B., et al. (1986). A qualitative analysis of categories of variables associated with professional satisfaction and dissatisfaction among middle school teachers. Paper presented at the Annual Meeting of the Mid-South Educational Research Association.

George, P.S. (1984). Middle school instructional organization: An emerging consensus. In J.H. Lounsbury (Ed.), *Perspectives on middle school education* (pp. 52-67). Columbus, OH: National Middle School Association.

George, P.S. & Oldaker, L.L. (1985). *Evidence for the middle school.* Columbus, OH: National Middle School Association.

Johnston, J.H. (1987). "Groups in Schools" paper presented at the National Association of Secondary School Principals' Middle Level Frontline Conference, Minneapolis, MN, November.

Levine, D.E., Levine, R.F., and Eubanks, E. (1984). Characteristics of successful inner-city intermediate schools, *Phi Delta Kappan, 65:* 707-711.

Lipsitz, J. (1984). *Successful schools for young adolescents.* New Brunswick, NJ: Transaction Books.

Little, J.W. & Bird, T. (1984). Report on a pilot study of school-level collegial teaming. (Contract No. 400-83-0003). Washington, D.C.: National Institute of Education. ED 266 540.

Since life is "interdisciplinary" at least some portion of the school curriculum should also be interdisciplinary if it is to help young people relate to life.

— Gordon Vars, 1987

The Effects of Teaming on Students

Joanne M. Arhar, J. Howard Johnston, Glenn C. Markle

Early research on this topic is limited and rather inconclusive but includes some claims of academic gains resulting from teaming.

Ultimately, the measure of any school practice must be whether it benefits the students that the school serves. The practice of interdisciplinary teaming is no exception. Thus, the purpose of this column is to examine research literature on the effects of interdisciplinary team teaching organizations on students, the ultimate consumers of educational services provided by the middle level school.

It is clear that teaming has important effects on the organizational climate, the satisfaction and professional development of teachers, and collaboration within the workplace. It is tempting, therefore, to conclude that any practice which has such wide-reaching influences in the school *must* affect student learning and school adjustment in equally potent ways.

Caution must be exercised in applying this logic, though. Teaming is an organizational change that *may* affect the way instruction is delivered in the school. It is also a way of restructuring human interaction among teachers, and possibly, among students, so that the school *can* become a collection of smaller, relatively cohesive groups. In other words, teaming creates an opportunity for things to be done differently in the school; it does not assure that they will. Therein lies the first problem: no organizational practice can guarantee that its major tenets will be implemented if the implementation depends upon the idiosyncratic decision of members of the organization to participate. And, while a team arrangement may allow collaboration to occur, it cannot compel it. Nor can it compel cross-disciplinary planning or instruction. As with all organizational concepts, teaming is at the mercy of the people who work on the teams.

Beyond the question of whether the major principles of teaming actually ever get implemented is the question of whether the implementation will affect the school's clients. Collaborative planning by teachers, a greater sense of camaraderie among staff and greater professional development among teachers are, themselves, desirable outcomes. Whether these outcomes have an effect on the nature of student learning, though, is a very different issue. Establishing links between organizational changes and operations is fairly straightforward; when organizations change, the things the organization does change as well. The links between an organizational change and the ultimate product of the organization are much more tenuous. So, while we can be almost certain that teaming changes how schools work, we cannot assume that those procedural changes alter the school's "product," student learning and behavior, in the same way.

23

Despite these questions, teaming is becoming the standard instructional organizational practice in the middle level school. George and Oldaker (1985) found that 90% of the sample in their study employed teaming in some form. Lounsbury and Johnston's (1988) study of the sixth grade indicated that 67% of the schools in the study used some form of teaming at the sixth grade. Clearly, because of its popularity, there is a strong *belief* among school people that teaming benefits the students. Is that belief rooted in empirical reality? The remainder of this column is devoted to that question.

Teaming and Student Achievement

Historically, teaming has shown little effect on student achievement. An early review of research on the subject (Armstrong, 1977) examined eleven studies conducted between 1959 and 1970. He concluded that "the relatively small number of studies on team teaching as it effects achievement may have resulted from the wide coverage given the innovation in professional journals in the late 1960s. This heavy media coverage may have planted the idea that this widely-heralded innovation sprang forth from a solid base of research evidence" (p. 79). Cotton's (1982) review of thirteen studies and three large-scale reviews to assess the effectiveness of team teaching in enhancing student achievement led her to conclude that "the research of the effectiveness of interdisciplinary team teaching, as compared with traditional, one-teacher/one-classroom arrangements, generally indicate that these two formats are equally effective in enhancing student achievement, both at the intermediate level and for students generally."

Contradictions are evident even among the studies cited in these reviews, however. Almost the same number of studies support traditional teaching as team arrangements. However, in virtually all cases where significant differences were found, other organizational arrangements, such as ability grouping, were present, or the measurements employed were locally produced (teacher-made tests, teacher grades, teacher ratings) and, therefore, subject to the effects of *beliefs* about teaming or traditional teaching that pervaded the local school setting.

Sinclair (1980) found that teaming produced significantly higher academic achievement on all areas of the California Achievement Test (CAT) among eighth graders. Georgiades and Bjelke (1966) found similar achievement differences, favoring team arrangements, on reading scores among ninth graders in three-period team arrangements. Jester (1965), on the other hand, found that traditional, departmentalized staffing was related to increased CAT scores in

> Teaming creates an opportunity for things to be done differently: it does not assure that they will be done.

> Teaming changes how schools work, but we cannot assume that those changes alter the school's "product," student learning and behavior, in the same way.

24

language arts, although no differences were found in social studies. Noto (1972) found that traditional, departmentalized arrangements produced higher achievement in math and reading as measured on the Iowa Test of Basic Skills. Sterns (1969), working with fourth and fifth graders, concluded that traditional one-teacher/one-class arrangements produced higher achievement as well.

Still, the vast majority of studies in this area report that there is no difference in student achievement as a result of team arrangements (Georgiades and Bjelke, 1964; Oakland Public Schools, 1964; Zimmerman, 1962; Gamsky, 1970; Cooper and Sterns, 1973). Thus, early research supported the position that conditions which tend to coexist with teaming or traditional arrangements, or some specific characteristics of students involved in the studies, have greater effect on student achievement than organizational arrangements *per se*.

More recently, the debate had been joined once again. Which arrangement produces higher achievement: teaming or traditional organization? George and Oldaker (1985) take the most assertive stance, saying that the findings from their study of one hundred particularly effective middle level schools "dispute earlier opinions that academic achievement is either unaffected or only modestly improved by a move to middle school organization. Rather than the typical finding of no differences, sixty-two percent of the respondents in this study described consistent academic improvement. An additional twenty-eight percent of the respondents supplied specific results demonstrating increased scores on state assessment tests, the California Achievement Test, the Iowa Test of Basic Skills, and similar tests since their schools became middle schools. An overwhelming majority, eighty-five percent, observed that teacher confidence in students' abilities had increased, which, many suggested, led to higher expectations and greater student productivity in academic classes" (p. 20).

In a study conducted in more controlled school settings, Bradley (1988) found, after studying seventh grade students in interdisciplinary teams and departmentalized arrangements, that the team arrangement was more effective "in fostering math achievement in seventh grade students." Further, both arrangements are equally effective in promoting reading achievement. She also found that, in general, students from all ability levels received higher mathematics achievement scores than did students in departmentalized settings. Team taught students from all ability levels did as well in reading as homogeneously grouped, departmentalized children.

Bradley's study is especially significant because it incorporates attention to the effects of grouping as it interacts with instructional

Conditions which coexist with teaming may have greater effect on achievement than the arrangement *per se*.

George and Oldaker claimed their study of effective schools shows an academic advantage from teaming.

organization to promote or inhibit student achievement. While the results are, at this point, suggestive, her work does indicate that greater research attention can be profitably spent on this interaction.

McPartland (1987) and McPartland, Coldiron, and Braddock (1987) compare achievement of sixth graders in self-contained and departmentalized settings and conclude that the self-contained setting is more effective for low ability students and no less effective than departmentalization for high-achieving students. Even after controlling for parent education level, school and community composition and school size, McPartland found that "teacher responsibilities for large numbers of students reduce their ability to attend to the special needs of individual students and specialized teachers are more likely to adopt a 'subject matter orientation' that emphasizes knowledge expertise than a 'student orientation' that emphasizes concern for individual students. Such an orientation affects student-teacher relationships and, consequently, student performance."

Some variations emerge in this data, though. Average test scores of students in departmentalized settings exceed those of self-contained students in two areas: science and social studies. Evidently, the more specialized subject matter is taught in a more specialized arrangement.

McPartland, however, does not examine team-taught settings. Instead, he postulates that "intermediate practices" (between self-contained and departmentalized) may work well for the middle level because it combines high-quality instruction from subject matter experts with specific attention to reducing student anonymity and building strong teacher-student relationships. One such arrangement that he cites is a team teaching; another is a homeroom or advisory program that permits the school to "compensate" for its attention to discipline-based instruction with a mechanism for enhancing the personal relationships between teachers and students.

Teaming and Affective and Social Outcomes

Advocates of middle level education programs in general and teaming in particular have long argued that a necessary goal for the middle level school is the affective and social development of children. In the past decade, these advocates have received support for this position from much of the research on school effectiveness, notably that of Rutter and his colleagues (1979). In *Fifteen Thousand Hours,* Rutter concludes that the two variables which seemed to differentiate between successful and unsuccessful inner city schools were the academic emphasis of the school *and* its psychosocial

> Sinclair found that there was a difference in student perception of school environment with team taught students finding the environment to be more supportive and facilitative.

environment. While the work of McPartland and his colleagues cited earlier gives credence to the academic emphasis dimension of Rutter's formula, other researchers have been more attentive to the psychosocial climate of the school and the extent to which organizational arrangements, particularly teaming, affect that environment.

Both Metz (1986) and Damico and colleagues (1981) found that teaming has an effect on interracial relationships in the school. White students reported having more black friends in team-organized schools than in traditional arrangements. Furthermore, white students' attitudes toward black students were significantly better in team arrangements. Black students' friendship patterns and attitudes were not significantly different as a result of school organization, but the trend in those data follow the same pattern as for the white students.

> **Teaming has a positive effect on interracial relationships.**

Metz' work speculated that faculty norms, teaching practices, and student attitude toward learning are all interrelated. In the schools which employed teaming, students expressed more enthusiasm about school and their teachers than did the students at the more traditional school (with departmentalized structure). Interracial cooperation in the classroom and interracial friendships were more common in the two team-organized schools. Conversely, racial tensions were more evident in the non-teamed school in this study. The staff at one of the teamed schools felt that low levels of conflict, which they attributed to the team structure, allowed them to help students cultivate their self-control and social responsibility. By modeling cooperative behavior, teachers felt that they were encouraging similar behavior on the part of their students. In contrast, teachers in the departmentalized school emphasized coverage of content rather than the social and group development in the class.

Sinclair (1980) found that there was a difference in student perception of school environment between teamed and departmentalized schools, with team-taught students finding the environment to be more supportive and facilitative. Gamsky (1970) found that team arrangement affected, positively, student attitude toward teachers, interest in subject matter, sense of personal freedom, and sense of self-reliance.

> **Improvements in school discipline result from teaming.**

George and Oldaker (1985) reported improvement in school discipline and student personal development as a result of their enrollment in middle schools, a principal component of which was team teaching. In general, they found that tardiness and truancy decreased as well as school vandalism and theft. "Approximately 80% (of the sample) noted significant reduction in office referrals and suspensions, while close to 60% expelled fewer students after the transition. Almost 90% observed that teacher and staff confidence in managing disruptive students increased, diminishing administrative involvement in discipline in many schools" (p. 31). One-fourth of their respondents gave anecdotal evidence specifically related to team organization. These respondents claimed that this organizational arrangement enabled teachers to develop consistent procedures for handling disruptions.

George and Oldaker (1985) also offer anecdotal evidence that teaming, in combination with the resulting teacher-based guidance that grows naturally from this arrangement, facilitated productive peer relationships and reduced conflict. Student emotional health, creativity, and confidence in self-directed learning, as well as student self-concept, were also positively affected.

George (1987) studied the long-term teacher-student relationships in a Florida middle school and found that the long-term relationships that resulted from a team arrangement in which students and teachers remain together for up to three years helped to improve discipline. George says that "teachers saw themselves as being much more willing to attempt behavior management alternatives when conventional or accustomed techniques failed to achieve the necessary results" (p. 10). They are less likely to use formalized, routine discipline procedures and were able to match both control strategies and consequences to the individual child. Both teachers and students agreed there was a stronger sense of student pride in their group and in their school as a whole. Students felt more self-confident, that they had more friends, that they "belonged" to the school and that they could be friends with all kinds of people.

Doda, writing in Ashton and Webb (1986), found that long-term, multiage grouping, often a feature of team arrangements, prevented teachers from "writing off" students who were difficult to teach. Because teachers knew that they would be working with the student over a longer time period than just one year, they were less willing to abandon efforts to reach a difficult child knowing that they would be "finished" with him or her at the end of the year. Middle school teachers tend to focus on long-term goals and tried to create an environment that encouraged student development and happiness.

As might be expected, all research conclusions are not consistent with those reported above. Odetola (1972) found that middle school students taught by team teaching methods were not necessarily less alienated from the school than those in traditional settings, and "the students taught by teacher teams indicated the greatest sense of powerlessness." Middle level students taught in conventional arrangements also gave the most positive responses to questions dealing with pride in or happiness with their schools. Sinclair (1980)

Teaming helped develop productive peer relationships and reduced conflict.

found no significant differences between students in team teaching arrangements and departmentalized arrangements in student attitudes toward their teachers.

Lipsitz (1984) studied four exceptionally successful middle level schools and found that they all used some variety of team arrangement. Ironically, the teachers in the school were not willing to attribute their success to any particular organizational arrangement. They were able to imagine that other, competing arrangements might be as successful, although satisfaction with the team arrangement was high. However, as Lipsitz concludes, "organizational ingenuity is possible in any school, reducing isolation by allowing for the small student focus groups and joint teacher planning time that characterize the four successful schools" (p. 200). Despite the fact that ingenuity is not confined to a given organizational type, it appears that the essential elements noted by Lipsitz seem to be characteristic of team arrangements.

Conclusion

Does teaming make a difference in student outcomes? The answer is that it probably does, but not in direct, easily discernible ways. It appears as if teaming is a manifestation of a commitment on the part of teachers to engage in teacher-student relationships that facilitate growth and individual student development. That teaming causes the philosophical commitment is unlikely; that it gives teachers the ability to translate this commitment into action is almost certain.

Furthermore, teaming does permit certain conditions to exist that are directly related to instructional effectiveness and student success. It reduces isolation and anonymity; it allows teachers to know their students quite well; and it permits teachers to "gang up" on students in positive ways to affect their learning. As Joan Lipsitz says, "organizational structure establishes continuity in adult-child relationships and opportunities for the lives of students and adults to cross in mutually meaningful ways. In each school, students express their appreciation for being cared about and known. They are actively aware of being liked, which is notable only because, in most schools, young adolescents are generally disliked" (p. 181).

NOTE: The authors wish to acknowledge their indebtedness to two dissertations that are particularly useful in understanding the context in which teaming occurs and the history of research in this area. Both are recommended for additional reading by those with a particular interest in team arrangements.

Teaming permits certain conditions to exist that are directly related to instructional effectiveness and student success.

Doda, Nancy M. (1984) Teacher perspectives and practices in two organizationally different middle schools. Unpublished Doctoral Dissertation, University of Florida, College of Education.

Bradley, Elizabeth M. (1988). The effectiveness of an interdisciplinary team organizational pattern compared with a departmentalized organizational pattern in a selected middle school setting. Unpublished Doctoral Dissertation, State University of New York, Buffalo, College of Education.

SEVEN NEW STUDIES OF TEAMING
Joanne M. Arhar

Seven new studies have been added to the growing list of significant contributions to our knowledge base on interdisciplinary teaming. Two look at the outcomes of teaming for teachers. Four examine the outcomes for students. And a seventh, a review of literature on the Pontoon Transitional Design, provides a historical perspective on the study of teaming. Together they take a hard look at the reality behind common beliefs about the values of teaming for middle level students and teachers.

Studies support the effectiveness of teaming for making teaching more appealing.

"The Influence of Interdisciplinary Teaming on Teacher Isolation" (Farris, Powell and Pollack, 1992), takes an inside look at three teams in Buckholder Junior High School and reveals some important insights into connectedness among teachers. Their qualitative study reveals that the isolation so characteristic of teachers' school lives is diminished within months after teams are formed. On the other hand, teaming allows other forms of isolation to occur — isolation from other teams and from one's own subject area department. Direct observation and interviews with teachers as they work on teams yield insights that are important to consider as we make decisions about how to structure our teams and departments.

Gatewood, Cline, Green and Harris in studying the middle school interdisciplinary team organization and its relationship to teacher stress (1992) hypothesized that teaming will reduce teacher stress. Their hypothesis is based on previous research which shows that stress is diminished by peer and supervisor support, control over working conditions, and enhanced personal sense of professionalism. The authors found that teaming did enhance a personal sense of professionalism among teachers.

Both studies of the outcomes of teaming for teachers support the effectiveness of this organizational pattern for making teaching a more appealing profession.

Stefanich, Mueller and Wills (1992) conducted a longitudinal study of interdisciplinary teaming and its influence on student self-concept. Self-concept has been positively associated with student performance and achievement, and thus is an important mediating variable for study. They found that self-concept was *not* affected by school organization. This contrasts an earlier study conducted by Stefanich (1980) in which teaming *was* associated with higher self-concept. However, self-concept scores improved overall in both teamed and non-teamed schools. The explanation they offer for their finding makes a great deal of sense in light of the progress we have made in middle level education over the last ten years toward achieving a child-centered focus.

Stefanich and colleagues also found that regardless of the number of years teams have been in place, teachers feel only minimal comfort with using it and subsequently do not implement it to its fullest potential for the improvement of curriculum and instruction. This disheartening news echoes the message from research on school restructuring: reorganization alone does not necessarily lead to substantive changes in the content of schooling.

Reorganizing alone does not necessarily lead to changes in the content of schooling.

In an attempt to discover if teaming in fact reduces the isolation and alienation students experience during early adolescence, Arhar (1992) examined the relationship between organizational arrangements (departmentalization and teaming) and students' sense of social bonding to teachers, peers, and school. A national sample of five thousand seventh graders, 2500 in teamed schools, and 2500 in non-teamed matched paired schools, completed a social bonding survey. Results indicate a significant difference favoring the teamed schools on bonding to teachers and to school and no difference on bonding to peers. Student relationships to peers most likely operates independent of the manner in which a school is organized for instruction.

Students in teamed schools had higher scores on bonding to peers and teachers than students in non-teamed schools.

In an ex post facto design (Arhar, in progress), the data from the earlier study were reanalyzed to explore the relationship between school organization (teamed and non-teamed) and student bonding to teachers, peers and school. Separate analyses were conducted for schools with a high percentage of students with low socio-economic status (SES) and schools with a high percentage of students with high SES backgrounds.

For the high SES schools, no statistically significant effects were obtained for school organization. In contrast, in the low SES schools, a statistically significant main effect was found for school organization. A follow-up test in the low SES schools indicated that students in teamed schools had significantly higher scores on bonding to peers

31

and bonding to teachers as compared to students in non-teamed school.

This study adds additional support for those urban, suburban, and rural schools with high concentrations of poor students to use inter-disciplinary team organization as a means to combat the sense of alienation experienced by students whose lives are fragmented by poverty.

McPartland (1991) used the recent national NELS:88 survey of over 24,000 eighth grade students and the supplemental survey of the principals of over 1,000 schools attended by these students to examine the effects of departmentalization and the effects of interdisciplinary teams on academic achievement and teacher-student relationships. As predicted, increased departmentalization (as measured by the number of different teachers each student has for the major subjects) "has negative effects on teacher-student relations. For the lowest SES group, the results were quite different. "For the lowest SES group, where the positive benefits of specialized teachers on achievement found for all other groups shift to negative on two of the four tests, raising questions of whether extensive departmentalization can be justified at all for the most needy students (p. 6).

He also found that the use of teams in highly departmentalized schools improved teacher-student relations and "does not detract from the positive academic effects of departmentalization, and may enhance these effects in social studies" (p. 8).McPartland's study supports the use of interdisciplinary teams in highly departmentalized schools as a means to offset the negative impact of departmentalization on teacher-student relations in semi-departmentalized schools (schools in which some teachers provide instruction in more than one subject) was still greater than relationships in highly departmentalized schools which use interdisciplinary teams. Together with Arhar's socio-demographic study, evidence suggests that teaming has both academic and social benefits for poor students.

Finally, Clark and Clark's review of studies of the Pontoon Transitional Design remind us that interdisciplinary teaming is not an innovation of the 1980s and 1990s. Its historical roots lie in part in the Pontoon Transitional Design, a comprehensive model of teaming that involved many elements now part of school restructuring — teacher decision-making, small communities of learners and teacher collaboration. In a thorough and carefully documented review of the literature of the Pontoon Transitional Design, they demonstrate how a research agenda can be built from earlier studies. Their review reminds us again that the work of middle school reformers leads the way in current restructuring efforts.

Restructuring middle level schools around the concept of inter-disciplinary teams is an idea that continues in the 1990s. Research on teaming that builds on the studies cited in these reviews and that examines the conditions, processes and effects of teaming as a major restructuring effort will continue to provide valuable information for practitioners as they try to make a fundamental impact on middle level schools. A research agenda based on the criteria for successful school restructuring (Arhar, 1992) offers promise for the improvement of the lives of both middle level teachers and their students. ▲

References

Armstrong, D.G. (1977). Team teaching and achievement. *Review of Educational Research, 47(1).*

Ashton, P.T., & Webb, R.B. (1986). *Making a difference: Teachers' sense of efficacy and student achievement.* New York: Longman, Inc.

Bradley, E.M. (1988). The effectiveness of an interdisciplinary team organizational pattern in a selected middle level school setting. Unpublished Doctoral Dissertation, State University of New York at Buffalo.

Calhoun, F. S. ((1983). *Organization of the middle grades: A summary of research.* Arlington, VA: Educational Research Service, Inc.

Cooper, D.H. & Sterns, H.N. (1973). Team teaching, student adjustment and achievement. *Journal of Educational Research, 66,* 323-327.

Cotton, K. (February 1982). *Effects of interdisciplinary team teaching, research synthesis.* Portland, OR: Northwest Regional Lab. ED 230533.

Damico, S. (1982). The impact of school organization of interracial contact among students. *Journal of Educational Equity and Leadership. 2,* 238-52.

Doda, N. M. (1984). Teacher perspectives and practices in two organizationally different middle schools. Unpublished Doctoral Dissertation, University of Florida.

Gamsky, N. (1970). Team teaching, student achievement and attitudes. *Journal of Experimental Education, 39,* 42-45.

George, P.S. (1987). *Long-term teacher-student relationships: A middle school case study.* Columbus, OH: National Middle School Association.

George, P.S. & Oldaker, L. L. (1985). *Evidence for the middle school.* Columbus, OH: National Middle School Association.

Georgiades, W. & Bjelke, J. (1964). Experiment in flexible scheduling of team teaching. *Journal of Secondary Education, 39,* 136-143.

Georgiades, W. & Bjelke, J. (1966). Evaluation of English achievement in a ninth grade three period team teaching class. *California Journal of Educational Research, 17(3),* 100-112.

Jester, J.F. Jr. (1966). A comparative study of the effects of team teaching and departmentalized teaching on scholastic achievement of eighth grade students in social studies and language arts. Unpublished Doctoral Dissertation, University of Kansas.

Lipsitz, J. (1984). *Successful schools for young adolescents.* New Brunswick, NJ: Transaction Books.

Lounsbury, J.H. & Johnston, J.H. (1988). *Life in the three 6th grades.* Reston VA: National Association of Secondary School Principals.

McPartland, J.M. (June 1987). *Balancing high quality subject matter instruction with positive teacher-student relations in the middle grades* (Report 15). Baltimore, MD: The Johns Hopkins University Center for Research on Elementary and Middle Schools.

McPartland, J.M., Coldiron, R. & Braddock II, J.H. (June 1987). *A description of school structures and classroom practices in elementary, middle, and secondary schools* (Report 14). Baltimore, MD: The Johns Hopkins University Center for Research on Elementary and Middle Schools.

Metz, M.H. (1986). *Different by design: The context and character of three magnet schools.* Routledge & Kegan Paul: New York.

Noto, R.E. (1972). A comparison between traditional teaching and interdisciplinary team teaching at the seventh grade level. Unpublished Doctoral Dissertation, St. Louis University.

Oakland Public Schools (1964). *Report of evaluation of special instructional programs at Madison Junior High School for years 1962-63 and 1963-64.* Oakland, CA.

Odetola, T. et al. (Winter 1972). Organizational structure and student alienation. *Educational Administration Quarterly, 8,* 15-26.

Rutter, M. et al. (1979). *Fifteen thousand hours: Secondary schools and their effects on children.* Cambridge, MA: Harvard University Press.

Sinclair, R. (1980). The effect of middle school staff organizational patterns on student perceptions of teacher performances, student perceptions of school environment and student academic achievement. Unpublished Doctoral Dissertation, Miami University.

Sterns, H.N. (1968). Student adjustment and achievement in a team teaching organization. Unpublished Doctoral Dissertation, University of Michigan.

Zimmerman, W.A. (1962). Departmental and unified seventh grade programs in English and social studies, a study of changes in subject matter achievement and personal adjustment. Unpublished Doctoral Dissertation, Syracuse University.

A survey by Paul George of 130 middle level schools that had been ranked as exemplary revealed that over 90% of those schools had interdisciplinary teams as a central feature. *(Evidence for the Middle School,* NMSA, 1985)

References for New Studies

Arhar, J.M. (1992) in J. Irvin (Ed.), *Transforming Middle Level Education.* Boston: Allyn and Bacon.

Arhar, J.M. The demographics of membership: Social variables affecting the bonding of at-risk youth. Manuscript in progress, University of South Florida, College of Education, Tampa.

Arhar, J.M. (1992). A research agenda for interdisciplinary teaming: Looking through the lens of restructuring. *Research in Middle Level Education, 15* (2). Columbus, OH: National Middle School Association.

Clark, S.N. & Clark, D.C. (1992). The pontoon transitional design: A missing link in the research on interdisciplinary teaming. *Research in Middle Level Education, 15* (2). Columbus, OH: National Middle School Association.

Farris, R.A., Powell, R.R. & Pollak, J.P. (1992). The influence of interdisciplinary teaming on teacher isolation: A case study. *Research in Middle Level Education, 15* (2). Columbus, OH: National Middle School Association.

Gatewood, T.E., Cline, G., Green, G., & Harris, S.E. (1992). Middle school interdisciplinary team organization and its relationship to teacher stress. *Research in Middle Level Education, 15* (2). Columbus, OH: National Middle School Association.

McPartland, J.M. (1991). *How departmentalized staffing and interdisciplinary teaming combine for effects on middle grades students.* Center for Research on Effective Schooling for Disadvantaged Students, Baltimore, MD: The Johns Hopkins University.

Stefanich, G.P. (1980). *Iowa Middle School Survey 1979-1980.* Cedar Falls, Iowa: University of Northern Iowa.

Stefanich, G.P., Mueller, J.C., Wills, F.W. (1992). A longitudinal study of interdisciplinary teaming and its influence on student self-concept. *Research in Middle Level Education, 15* (2). Columbus, OH: National Middle School Association.

> We need to break the illusion of separate subjects. Education is about life. Life is a fabric of relationships — the child should grasp this through his experience. Subjects which break off areas of knowledge and set up as independent islands have deceptive powers. Traditional teaching of subjects ... is death to the understanding.
>
> — Peter Abb (1966)

DIFFERENCES BETWEEN MORE PRODUCTIVE
AND LESS PRODUCTIVE TEAMS

A comprehensive research study by Dr. Nancy Bell of Shorter College, Rome, Georgia, compared "more productive" teams with "less productive" teams. Based on extensive visits, personal observations, interviews, and study of records, descriptions of more productive and less productive teams were developed in three categories.

	More effective teams	Less effective teams
Leadership	Appreciated the efforts of county officials	Tended to view county level personnel as those who forced them to work together.
	Team leaders communicated, often with administrators and with teammates.	Team leaders communicated less with administrators and with teammates.
	Team leaders were competent, supportive, and respected by team members. They were knowledgeable, enthusiastic, and organized.	Team leaders did not believe they received support from administrators or team members.
Communication	Commitment to the middle school philosophy by at least two team members.	Only one team member evidences commitment to the middle school philosophy.
	Members were very willing to share responsibilities.	Team meetings were mundane and members' attitudes were negative.
	Spent more time talking about students which led to agreed-upon follow-up actions.	Spent less time talking about students and often do not decide upon any action.
Structure	Leaders provided team with typed agenda	Agenda, if existed, only handwritten.
	Team members had assigned responsibilities.	No assigned duties for individuals.
	Meetings were held around a table, refreshments often available.	Members disinterested, often graded papers during team meeting.

Are Interdisciplinary Units Worthwhile? Ask Students

Mary A. Davies

Five years of student evaluations validated the use of units, provided clues for future plans, and increased student involvement.

Educational practices call for frequent evaluation and reflection to insure their effectiveness. Students, as the consumers, are a logical source of evaluative responses. Yet all too often, educators neglect to ask students questions about their perceptions of instructional effectiveness.

The purported benefits of interdisciplinary units have long been lauded amongst middle level advocates; but limited data exist to support the merits of this instructional approach. In order to begin filling this void, student feedback on interdisciplinary units was collected over a five-year period. After each unit, students responded to a brief Likert-type questionnaire. They indicated their level of agreement with five statements, rated their projects and offered evaluation comments. These self-report data provide guidance for structuring interdisciplinary units and support several important middle level goals. Altogether some 700 sixth, seventh, and eighth grade students provided responses to the questionnaire.

Evaluation Questions and Responses

Imagine a classroom where students enthusiastically engage in learning, and upon completion of a study they express that they learned a great deal and cannot wait until the next unit. Sound too good to be true? This scenario however, reflects a frequent reaction to interdisciplinary instruction. Student evaluations provide insights as to why interdisciplinary units successfully promote learning .

Item one on the evaluation instrument asked students to indicate their level of agreement with the statement, "The topic was interesting to me." Only one topic received less than 80% positive agreement. Interest in the topic seemed to fuel motivation to learn. Students were periodically polled concerning interdisciplinary topics they would like to investigate. These suggestions guided the selection of future units.

Student responses to the second item, "I felt I learned something," revealed a high level of agreement. On the average, 95% of all students agreed or strongly agreed with this statement. Interestingly, the topic with the lowest positive interest level, Eastern Europe (75%), received the highest perceptions of having learned something (99%). It was probably the least familiar topic, and this fact contributed to perceptions of having learned more.

What elements of interdisciplinary structure fostered perceptions of learning? One related factor was the degree of organization within a unit. The more clearly the goals and objectives were conveyed to students and developed through congruent activities, the more they felt they learned.

The very nature of interdisciplinary instruction also enhanced understanding. This approach developed a topic from the perspectives of several disciplines (team composition varied). The process of linking and elaborating upon ideas reinforced them.

The interaction of these and other factors promoted learning. Incorporating varied activities, offering choices, integrating skill development with content, and providing many opportunities for hands-on experiences actively involved students in finding meaning.

Another common component of all interdisciplinary units was the opportunity for students to share their project/knowledge with others. The audiences varied and may have included other team members, elementary students, peers and other teams, and parents. Sharing provided a forum for practicing listening and verbal communication skills and learning the value of each individual's knowledge. Although these are difficult areas to master, student feedback revealed progress in these areas.

The third statement on the instrument assessed the perceived effectiveness of the sharing. With one exception, over eighty percent of the responses for all units indicated some level of agreement with this statement, "I felt I learned something from the sharing of projects." The comparatively low positive response rating for the "Signs of the Times" unit (67%) was likely attributable to the fact that students shared their projects on the last full day of the school year and the main focus of the unit had been the development of a research paper.

In contrast, the high percentage of "strongly agree" responses for the "Colonial America" unit probably resulted from use of a different structure. Rather than investigating/creating a project or writing a research paper, students studied a selected aspect of colonial life (e.g., leisure activities, religion, education). They then guided others in recreating that aspect of colonial life during a twenty-four hour simulation of colonial America. Overall, feedback supported sharing in different modes as a viable means of extending learning.

All interdisciplinary units incorporated large and small group activities. This reflected the common goal of assisting early adolescents in developing positive peer interactions. Students worked collaboratively in groups of two to four on independent projects. Groups were both teacher and self-selected. The evaluations sent

> "I felt I learned something." Ninety-five percent of all students agreed or strongly agreed with this statement.

> The opportunity for students to share their knowledge with others provided a forum for practicing communication skills.

home upon completion of each unit included the criterion "cooperation with others." Thus, the important middle level goal of positive peer interactions was reinforced by providing guidance in collaborative skill development, practice opportunities and feedback.

Responses to "I worked well with others" showed growth in the area of interpersonal relations. On the average, ninety-four percent of the students in all units agreed or strongly agreed with this statement. The comments of two team members underscored the importance of varied groupings. "I learned that I like(d) working with myself and other people." "I made new friends and became better friends with others."

Interdisciplinary instruction definitely sparked an interest in learning. Responses to "I enjoyed this unit" revealed an average agreement rate of eighty-four percent. Many factors contributed to this enjoyment. Teacher enthusiasm generated student enthusiasm. The teachers loved the challenge of trying to make each unit different and exciting. All units included at least one field trip, a variety of activities, active involvement, and opportunities for choice-making. Learning became an exciting and challenging participatory activity!

The last item on the evaluation asked students to rate their own project or participation. The five category rating scale ranged from poor to excellent. Eighty-seven percent of the ratings for all units fell into the good, very good, or excellent categories. Overall, students expressed satisfaction with the quality of their work. Work well done reaped the benefits of personal pride and higher self-esteem.

Making Interdisciplinary Units Work

Students' open ended comments provided further feedback on the interdisciplinary units. They mentioned what they really liked and disliked about each unit — their unbridled honesty providing helpful insights into effective interdisciplinary approaches. These comments and our own observations combined to create the following list of tips.

Successful interdisciplinary units should include:

1. **Relevant topics.** Students enjoyed units more if they perceived a direct relevance to their lives. Solicit student input on topics and involve them in planning units.

2. **Clear goals and objectives.** Student perceptions of learning correlated positively with the degree of organization and structure in each unit. The more clearly the goals and objectives were conveyed to students, the more they felt they learned. Keep the use of time flexible, however.

> "I learned that I like working with myself and other people."

> "I made new friends and became better friends with others."

> Students expressed satisfaction with the quality of their work — they reaped the benefits of personal pride and higher self-esteem.

3. Variety in topics, activities, grouping. Attempt to structure each unit differently. Integrate a variety of activities into the unit, e.g., individual/group research, project construction, simulations, guest speakers, field trips, presentations, interviews, and surveys. Provide for individual, large, and small group activities.

4. Choice in topics, projects, groupings. Include opportunities for student input and options, thereby increasing motivation and fostering a sense of responsibility for one's learning.

5. Adequate time. Allow sufficient time to explore and incubate ideas, practice skills, and complete all work with pride.

6. Processes and/or products. Weave skill development into unit topic (e.g., developing, administering, tabulating, and graphing a survey on attitudes toward work in World of Work unit). Use products as vehicles for further student exploration of a topic.

7. Field trips. Take students on field trips that enable them to "experience" the topic. Assist them in seeing opportunities for learning beyond school walls.

8. Group cooperation. Incorporate group work. Possible ways to facilitate positive peer interactions include: committee work (e.g., planning for and assisting at open house), group projects, group tasks (e.g., survey design, administration and analysis), and group sharing.

9. Sharing. Have students share their knowledge/projects with others, e.g., invite another team, an elementary class, or parents. Public sharing encourages quality work, reinforces learning, and conveys that all contribute to the teaching/learning process.

10. Community involvement. Involve parents and community members as resource people, chaperones, and aides. This expands students' views of learning, allows greater flexibility of grouping and structure, and builds a bridge between school and community.

Interdisciplinary Links

Each statement on the evaluation form interacts with the others, reflecting the actual complexity of the learning process. Although this article analyzes each item separately for the sake of clarity, the statements are closely linked. If the topic is perceived as interesting, students get mentally involved, exert effort, produce quality work, learn more, and feel satisfied with their performance. This cycle is self-reinforcing. Students who actively participate and enjoy a unit tend to look forward to the next unit. And the cycle continues . . .

> **Students enjoyed units more if they perceived a direct relevance to their lives.**

> **Public sharing of projects encourages quality work, reinforces learning, and conveys that all contribute to the teaching/learning process.**

An apple analogy illustrates the interactive levels present. The outer skin of the apple leads the consumer to make judgments about the quality of the inside. So too in the classroom, teachers make inferences about student learning based on observed behaviors. The teacher notes signs of enjoyment, quality of work, peer interactions, and other evaluative data. Inside the apple, the flesh tastes good and nourishes. Similarly, inside the learner interest (linked to prior knowledge) excites and motivates the student to expend energy and process information. This "feeds" learning. Just as each apple seed contains potential for new growth if given the proper support environment, ideas learned hold the potential for continued expansion and independent learning. Interdisciplinary instruction plants the seeds.

Conclusion

As educators, we often "sense" which teaching practices seem to promote learning. By securing student feedback on our teaching, we translate this "sense" into concrete data. Several benefits emerge from this process.

1. Students take a more active role in learning when given opportunities for direct involvement in evaluating processes and activities.

2. Student suggestions give clues for the structuring of future units. They clarify the effective and ineffective components of instruction.

3. Students' assessments provide data to support interdisciplinary instruction as a viable middle school component.

4. Student evaluation data validate an interdisciplinary approach in the eyes of parents and the broader community and serve to build community support for middle schools.

The integrative nature of interdisciplinary units encourages students to "see" the interconnectedness of the world around them. This linking renders the world more relevant by connecting content, self, and community. Understanding the links generates excitement and fuels the desire to know more. Student comments capture this enthusiasm—they should be solicited. ▲

Evaluation data validate an interdisciplinary approach in the eyes of parents and the broader community.

Student comments capture the enthusiasm—they should be solicited.

From *Turning Points: Preparing American Youth for the 21st Century* Carnegie Council on Adolescent Development, Carnegie Corporation of New York (1989).

A better approach than departmentalization is to create teams of teachers and students who work together to achieve academic and personal goals for students. Teachers share responsibility for the same students and can solve problems together, often before they reach the crisis stage; teachers report that classroom discipline problems are dramatically reduced through teaming. This community of learning nurtures bonds between teacher and student that are the building blocks of the education of the young adolescent.

———————

The core middle grade curriculum can be organized around integrating themes that young people find relevant to their own lives. For example, separate courses in English, arts, history, and social studies might be grouped into the humanities, organized around an integrating theme such as Immigration. Mathematics and science could be combined in the study of themes such as Mapping the Environment.

SECTION II

Planning for Interdisciplinary Instruction

Doda   **Nancy Doda,** Educational Consultant, Burke, VA

Levy   **Phyllis Saltzman Levy,** formerly a teacher in Upper Arlington Schools, Columbus, OH.

Heck   **Shirley F. Heck,** Professor Emeritus and Head of Discovery School, Ohio State University, Mansfield, OH

Worsham   **Toni Worsham,** Professor of Education and Director of the Maryland Center for Thinking Studies, Coppin State College, Baltimore, MD

Maute   **Joan Maute,** Staff Development Coordinator for Indian Prairie School District #204 and sixth grade social studies teacher, Naperville, IL

Teaming:
Its Burdens and Its Blessings

NANCY DODA

Based on her extensive experience, the author
answers the question, "What really makes a team work?"

Teaming can be both a burden and a bless-ing. In theory, it is a joining, connecting, and collaborating arrangement. In practice, it is too often like a poorly run small business — per-haps well stocked, but somehow unable to thrive. While many teachers have been the lucky recipients of carefully planned and help-ful staff development opportunities intended to prepare them for a teaming experience, most would agree that you've really got to live it to know it. From the teacher's perspective, it is often only in the context of a working team, that one can discover the realities and possibilities; burdens and blessings of teaming. So it is that the majority of the insights and recommenda-tions that follow have come from the field of practicing teams who have shared their stories of both struggle and success, in order that future teams will have even better stories to tell in the years of ahead.

The Blessings

The act of organizing students and teachers into smaller, more personal communities makes sense for young adolescents in the middle grades. After all, most departmentalized sec-ondary schools are large and anonymous insti-tutions where teacher-student relationships are largely left to chance, and where students fre-quently move among seven different teachers, who work independently in seven different areas of the school. In a team organized middle level school, where any configuration of two or more teachers from varying disciplines are organized to share the instructional responsi-bility for a given population of learners, stu-dents can be members of a small knowable group which is both physically and interper-sonally more intimate. In such a structure, vulnerable young adolescents can become the recipients of the collective and collaborative caring efforts of several teachers who have a mutual interest in their success. Furthermore, in cross-discipline discussions of students, teachers are better able to know and understand students as whole learners from a variety of perspectives. For students, this increased teacher knowledge translates into a sense of being known and owned.

Being known well as a learner is an enor-mous boon to the academic initiative and suc-cess of middle school students. Reluctant learn-ers in particular, tend to respond more favor-ably to adults with whom they have had more than a random schedule of contacts. In listening to students, some have even confessed that being part of a team often means being known and owned in ways that deter deviance. While visiting Northside Middle School in Norfolk,

Virginia, a student on the S.W.A.T. (Students With Awesome Talent) team said that the only shortcoming of the team plan was that his, "... teachers were ganging up on him." It is, however, precisely this dynamic which gives teaming teachers the opportunity to powerfully and positively alter the learning environment and the course of their students' school experiences.

Since teachers share the same students and the associated challenges of teaching them, an additional blessing is that teams are often moved to cultivate a consistent environment for their students, including shared expectations, common supply requirements and shared approaches to discipline and instruction. For the emerging young adolescent, simplicity and order can be extremely helpful as they struggle to manage the increased demands of school life. Moreover, for teachers themselves, this shared vision provides a supportive and useful frame of reference as they deal with common dilemmas in teaching.

A student said...

The Team is a place where no one gets away with anything.

To which I added...

The Team is a place where no one is a stranger.

While the academically related affective benefits are fairly obvious, it is imperative that middle level educators recognize the powerful curricular and instructional reform potential hidden in the team structure. After years of important preparatory work, many teams remain fixed in a departmentalized arrangement in which very little innovation occurs in the nature of curriculum or instruction. When fully developed, the team organization should facilitate curriculum integration and responsive instructional planning.

Finally, teaming has additional rewards that benefit teachers in often unimagined ways. Few teachers realize before they engage in a teaming experience, that being part of a teaching team can work to bolster their professional confidence and conviction. Given the day to day difficulties teachers face in the classroom, with parents, with school limitations and even fellow staff, it is not uncommon for professional fervor to fade. Working on a team with colleagues who share the same students makes it possible for teachers to view problems encountered with realism and support. No longer is a difficult dilemma viewed entirely as a personal failure. It can be realistically understood and collectively resolved.

It is indeed delightful to acknowledge the dividends of teaming. Unfortunately, not all teams have the chance to enjoy them. How can teams experience the blessings and avoid the burdens ?

Organizing Teams for Success: Avoiding the Burdens

The practice of teaming is certainly not a new educational idea, nor is its application limited to middle level educational settings. As a result, there is an ever-growing body of testimony from the field which offers guidance on the successful organization and operation of teams. Fortunately, albeit recently, there is an equally emerging body of research which is serving to further enlighten our practice of teaming in the middle level school. From both the voice of practitioners and research, we now have a fairly clear list of organizing guidelines which delineate certain basics which ought to exist if authentic teaming is to flourish.

Staffing

Perhaps first and by far most obvious, teams within a school ought to have balanced teacher populations where teachers of contrasting strengths, personalities, instructional expertise and teaching experience are pooled together in order to teach a common group of students. Though teacher differences are essential for rich teaming endeavors, they are bound to produce the kind of conflict which can often endanger the health and longevity of teams. Some degree of conflict is inevitable in collaborative endeavors, but success in managing such conflict may be the single most critical factor in the wellness of any team.

Decisions regarding the actual composition of team staff are rarely unencumbered. Generally, subject area/ grade level certification impact where particular teachers are placed. Where flexibility does exist in the staffing of teams, it is helpful to collect data on teachers' perceptions of any persons on staff with whom they feel they could not work well, as well as any persons on staff with whom they feel they could work well. In this way, severe conflicts are potentially avoidable.

Even where teachers appear to be initially satisfied with their team assignments, it is prudent to pay close attention to whole school hospitality. Teaming teachers frequently report that they have insufficient time to connect with colleagues outside of their teams . In extreme cases, such individuals who are particularly unhappy with this, may unintentionally sabotage the team dynamics with a bitter twist of regret. Moreover, it is equally useful to build into the staff development blueprint, a long-term plan for continued work on team dynamics. Balancing personalities successfully does not seem to be as important as enabling staff to discuss their differences with respect and tolerance. Many school have found it therapeutic to schedule a retreat for staff as they move into the early years of their teaming experience.

While these suggestions are applicable to all teams, there seems to be growing evidence which suggests that smaller teams have fewer internal conflicts and increased longevity. Given the predominance of single subject secondary certification, however, the majority of middle

Teams should have a balanced staff with varying strengths and personalities.

Evidence suggests that smaller teams have fewer internal conflicts and increased longevity.

school teams are comprised of four subject area specialists. As plans are drafted for the shapes of your teams, explore the possibility of two or three teacher teams, in which the teamed teachers would share a smaller number of students and one or two additional subject area preparations. Many middle school teachers have confessed that they would prefer to teach two different subjects on a three teacher team to 85 students, rather than teach one subject to 120 students. In addition, smaller teaching teams are far more likely than larger teams, to embrace curriculum integration and the flexible use of the daily schedule.

Configurations

The grouping and scheduling of students may be even more challenging. Striving to create whole teams that have heterogeneous student populations often challenges components of school life that were once deemed untouchable. If the primary goal is to create teams which are balanced according to sex, intelligence, race, exceptionalities, and participation in the band program, then no single team should have all of any one kind of student, nor should team populations be skewed by any discriminating variable or program participation. In many schools, all of the band students have travelled together in order to accommodate the performance schedule. This would no longer be possible if teams are to have balanced student populations. Where schools are forced to place any single population of students on a team, it is imperative that other shuffling of students occur in order to balance the intellectual composition of the teams.

Second to my concern for balance is the need for physical distinction. The critical development of team identity is tremendously facilitated when the teams are housed in separate and distinct locations in a school. In a traditional building, where classrooms are only connected by an adjoining hallway, it is advisable to have teaming teachers in neighboring classrooms so that an entire team of students and teachers are close throughout most of the school day. Quite often, this shifting of space reeks havoc with sentiments about the enterprise of teaming, and yet most teachers will generously report that space matters. If nothing else, the creation of team areas reduces random and weakly supervised hallway traffic, exchanged for more controlled movement in team areas.

As Winston Churchill once said, "We shape our institutions and thereafter they shape us." Common team space is as important for teachers as for students. Where teaming teachers have a place for planning, meeting, storing and refueling, teams tend to feel empowered and connected. After all, if the central unit for instructional planning is the team, then space for planning should strive to accommodate that unit.

Teams ought to be as balanced as possible according to intelligence, sex, race, and exceptionalities.

Teams should be housed in separate and distinctive locations.

Communications

In order for teams to be fully functioning communities for teachers and students, team autonomy must exist. But it must exist in the context of a vital and solid school community. Perhaps one of the more treacherous traps of teaming, is the assumption that teams can work independent from the whole. Too often teachers find themselves inadvertently thrown into unhealthy team competition, when a single team is perceived by students as having a superior edge. Balance depends on effective communication and collaboration among teams, so that autonomy is negotiated within the context of some agreed upon parameters. Most often, schools have relied upon a model of team leadership for communication among teams. Team leaders, or team facilitators, usually selected by the school administration or voted in by experienced team members, provide the team with guidance and direction as they organize team meetings and events, facilitate better teaming relations, function as a check on team instructional programs and plans, and represent the team in school policy making and cross team collaboration.

While team leaders need to remain connected, it is absolutely essential that our non-teamed staff remain connected as well. In some middle schools, staff who teach outside the core teams, feel left out and disengaged from the teaming process. Certainly, team attachments that incorporate all staff are helpful, and yet communication and inclusion matter most. When teams host parent or student conferences, affiliated staff should be included. If at all possible, they should be present and if attendance is impossible, some written input should be gathered by the participating team or alternative meeting times explored. When our specialists are not actively engaged in sharing their perceptions about students, we lose a tremendous resource in understanding our students as whole learners. Insights about a child's brilliance in art can only be helpful to us as we plan for the continued growth and development of that child in all curriculum areas.

These suggestions to promote authentic teaming are more specifically intended to provide teachers and administrators with a vision about some of the prerequisites necessary for establishing teaming communities. Without the basics, teaming becomes more a burden to be cast aside than a blessing to be cherished.

Ways to Team: Reaping the Blessings

Fully functioning teams are not only organizationally sound; they are operationally productive. They mobilize themselves in ways that make the very most of the team arrangement for planning and teaching and that yield wonderful dividends for themselves, students and parents. While there is no single formula for ways to team, many teams have found that decisions about what is most important to do,

> In order for teams to be fully functioning communities for teachers and students, team autonomy must exist.

> Non-teamed staff need to be connected in some ways.

should evolve from an understanding of the critical core needs of their team's students. In other words, before planning a dozen ways to team, it is in the best interest of the team's growth, to first identify what students will need in order to be successful. With limited planning time, it is imperative to delineate what matters most so that teams operate from a core set of assumptions about where to spend their time and resources.

While variations in team missions produce diversity in team activities, many teams have experimented with plans in the following areas: Team Climate/Identity, Team Management, and Team Instruction. In most cases, beginning teams find Climate and Management decisions far less cumbersome than decisions in the area of Instruction. Consequently, it is not uncommon for teams to work together for a couple of years before venturing into the arena of Instructional Coordination and Integration.

Team Identity

Do students have a sense that they are a part of a team community? Are team areas made visible and distinct by their decor, activities, and climate? Even in team organized middle level schools, teaming is not always advertised to students. In fact, some students are not at all aware that they have been placed on an interdisciplinary team. If teaming is to have the power to make large schools feel smaller and more personal, then students will need to witness that sense of smallness. In building team identity, teams should work to target at least some of the following goals: familiarity within the team community, pride in the team, a sense of belonging, and enhanced teacher-students relationships. Examples might include:

(a) **Team Field Trip** —A team must work to become a group and field trips provide a perfect opportunity for group cohesiveness. Involving students in the plans and preparing some team-wide pre-trip and post-trip experience-related activities can add another dimension. If advisory time is connected with the team, advisors can use this time to coordinate the related activities.

(b) **Team Recognition** — Recognizing team achievements is a team pride booster. For Honor Roll, posting the names of students in a common team area and even awarding special buttons or certificates or privileges is encouraging. In one team, the students enjoyed a team honor roll "Smarty Party" with refreshments. Hosting several team awards assemblies throughout the year is a way to recognize a broad cross-section of students for a variety of successes. Some teams have weekly recognition for very specific behaviors they are hoping to encourage. Others have semester ceremonies to acknowledge civic and academic accomplishments. Most importantly, the team structure

A sense of team spirit is like a magic key which unlocks valuable doors with middle school kids.

should enable teachers to know students well enough to discover, uncover and celebrate the unique accomplishments of each and every student on the team.

(c) **Team Projects** — There are many community service learning projects which could involve an entire team. Projects designed for needy local groups are a wonderful way to engage a team in unified effort. Moreover, many teams have delighted in the chance to conduct performances in order to entertain, raise monies, or simply display learnings.

(d) **Team Gatherings** — Regularly scheduled team meetings where all team community members and teachers carry on a planning or ideas session captures an aspect of teaming often overlooked. The physical gathering plus the total team involvement in team affairs says to kids that the team is theirs and their participation counts.

(e) **Team Sports** — Middle school intramural athletics is an exciting way to foster team spirit. Lots of kids can partake and the entire team provides cheering support. Some teams even have practice games in various sports to get ready for the competition. Coordination might take place through the physical education program or advisory time.

Team Communication.

Constant and effective communication is essential between the team teachers and team students and/or parents. At the opening of every school year it is advisable to set the mode by planning and executing a thorough team orientation. A team orientation serves to introduce new middle school students to the notion of a team, while acquainting all students with the team staff, schedule, and general proceedings. This notion could be extended to a Team Back to School Night in which parents can experience the team feeling.

Individual student and team conferences are helpful throughout the year. When a child needs special guidance and support in setting academic goals for personal growth, an entire team can meet with the student to advise, guide and assist. Often a team will write up a contract to be agreed upon by the student and all of his cooperating teachers. The contract can then meet all of the student's needs academically without presenting a conflict with another teacher's expectations or plans. The child is able to receive help from a four way support system.

Teaming teachers can embrace students by embracing their parents. Team parent conferences provide the parent with multiple perspectives on their child's performance. Moreover, when several

> Constant communication is essential between students, teachers, and parents.

51

teachers offer the same recommendations or draw similar conclusions, parents are drawn to examine issues they may have otherwise approached with reservation concerning their child. Parents are also delighted when they receive a team newsletter sharing information about the instructional activities of the team or when they are invited to participate in one of the team's many special events.

Providing avenues for student-to-team communication is usually handled in less formal ways. Students talk to teachers, but nevertheless lots of good suggestions go by the wayside. A large "Red Hot Idea Box" helps if students are encouraged to use it freely. Some teams even have monthly Team Community Meetings where governance issues are managed.

Team Management

Teams frequently report that the most obvious blessing teaming provides is that of improved classroom discipline. No doubt, consistency across the team means a safer, more orderly environment for teachers and students. Many teams have discovered that it is helpful to have simple and common expectations for students. Others have found that having a simple and common supply list can mean fewer lost or disheveled papers and notebooks. Still others have noted that creating a team calendar for all major homework projects and tests can facilitate responsibility and planning for both students and teachers and also eliminate the problem of overlapping homework.

Improved discipline is an obvious blessing of teaming.

In planning for effective discipline, it is wise to spend some time discussing philosophies and practices in an effort to understand what each team member brings to the development of the team's plan. The hope is that the resulting plan for team discipline will be the finest blend of individual ideas and successful practices. It is particularly helpful if teachers can agree on several general ways to manage and respond to common dilemmas. Finally, many teams work exceedingly hard to find dozens of ways to catch students being good, and to acknowledge these positively. Examples in the management domain might include:

(a) **Team Conferences** — A team might choose to invite several exemplary citizens to a team conference where the only purpose is to thank these celebrated students for their fine behavior and participation. Imagine the effect on the team's climate when you have clusters of students who have been properly appreciated. Of course, teams can also meet with struggling students to draft therapeutic plans for their improvement. Such team conferences might lead to special plans such as weekly progress checks sent home, after school assistance, daily behavior contracts, or meetings with the Lunch Study Bunch held in the team area.

(b) Team Organizational Tools — If teams can manage to draft a calendar for students which includes their collective major assignments for a semester, this master plan can help students plan ahead, enable parents to coach at home, and help team teachers monitor the workload for the term. Many teams find students benefit from a specific system of notebook organization, and work to develop a team plan to that effect. One or two notebooks are far more manageable than five or six. Finally, as an interdisciplinary initiative, teams can arrange to integrate study skills in all they do. This provides a set of consistent tools that all students can master.

Team Instruction

While in all the domains of teaming the possibilities are nearly endless, the complexity of options in the instructional domain often seem overwhelming. In fact, many teachers find themselves reticent to team because they envision the instructional challenges to be far too demanding. And in some cases, this may very well be true. In order for effective instructional teaming to occur, teachers must be afforded a daily unencumbered team planning period, coupled with staff development opportunities designed to assist teachers in the use of this time for planning.

Many teams have found that they can start slowly and increase their instructional level of teamwork over time. Small but engaging team experiences can be constructed such as a single day's interdisciplinary celebration of a social studies theme. A Medieval Day or Colonial Day might serve to culminate a unit of study with all teachers participating in its preparation and execution.

Equally small but significant would be a two teacher plan to integrate a project assignment or several lessons on a related topic. Reading selections or writing activities for English can easily connect with science or social studies, as the assignments encourage students to weave together their learnings from all disciplines. Moreover, a whole team could easily create a vocabulary list rather than continue to teach subject segregated vocabulary or spelling.

Without question, full interdisciplinary units involving all areas of study are more challenging. The classic interdisciplinary unit often involves all core subjects in planning and works through a single theme. It is important to caution teams that many thematic units run the risk of being more entertaining than instructional. Too often clever themes can obscure instructional substance. If the theme makes it possible for students to enrich and deepen their understandings of the proposed concepts and ideas or to master the projected outcomes, then it has potential. Otherwise, it is best to dig deeper for another theme which will work to instruct as well as entertain.

> **Many thematic units run the risk of being more entertaining than instructional.**

When planning any unit which attempts to integrate, it is exceedingly helpful to work from a master grid of proposed outcomes or goals. Some teams find it useful to create semester briefs which list each teacher's agenda of primary concepts, topics, skills or outcomes. Using the completed grid, the team is then able to identify any apparent connections across the curriculum or what have been called, "lucky links" in an effort to plan for integration. With more experienced teams who are hoping to move towards a comprehensive plan for integration, a master plan for the whole school year might be generated and applied to the year's planning process. With the recent movement to outcomes based planning, many schools have encouraged teams to plan for outcomes based integration. In this way, integrated efforts focus on the collaborative teaching of outcomes and not specific content. Ultimately, while this is still a prescribed curriculum, it is less likely to run the risk of being merely entertaining, and has an increased chance of engaging many subjects across the school day.

Clarifying proposed goals and outcomes is important in planning any unit.

While increasing numbers of teams are experimenting with curriculum integration, many more remain stuck within the confines of subject-centered teaching. An equal number remain captives of the traditional period by period conception of instructional time. Without flexibility in the grouping and scheduling of students as well as freedom to manipulate time as needed for team planned instruction, many teams have difficulty evolving towards increased integration.

Teams need to capitalize on opportunities to alter time and student groupings.

Simple efforts to alter the day's schedule are beginning to emerge. A team might, for instance, show a film to all of the team's students during a block of time and simply adjust the length of the remaining class periods accordingly. This eliminates the need to show that film for five consecutive class periods in one subject. It further enhances the chance that the team's teachers would coordinate a follow-up lesson that same day. These are often the beginning steps needed before teams are willing to move towards larger undertakings which literally turn the day's schedule and traditional student groupings upside down. If teams did plan units of study which centered on themes generated from students' interests, concerns and questions, and worked to integrate the subjects as resources useful in addressing these themes, then planning for lessons, the grouping of students, and use of time take on new meanings. Such heightened levels of flexibility are still the exception, but the strength of conviction about the merits of such an approach is building, and most certainly predicts the direction in which our integrating efforts will move.

Reflections

Classroom teaching has changed dramatically over the past several decades. The social forces affecting our emerging young adolescents continue to place our students at risk of school failure as well as personal devastation. Students confront grave decisions at earlier ages and do so often with less support from either families or society at large. Many children face school with depleted personal resources, diminished motivation, or poor health. In harmony, teachers struggle often against incredible odds to make a difference in the lives of the students they meet and teach each year. If teachers are to remain cloistered behind closed doors, unaided by colleagues who must likewise struggle alone, teachers will also be at continued risk of professional defeat. At the middle level, in particular, but in any school, collaborative teaching among all staff must prevail. The time for going it alone is over, and though working together involves compromise, sacrifice, tolerance, and dialogue, the blessings most definitely surpass the burdens, for ourselves, the children we teach today and for the generations to follow.

My suggestions are not meant to provide a one-way route to better teaming. They should, however, share my reflections on teaming in a practical way. I am still left with one last thought and that is that no matter how much we want to do for kids we can only do so much. As you consider all of these suggestions, consider too that teaming is hard work and may mean working with others we may not like. It means additional time for planning and communication, and maybe giving much more of ourselves than we may be accustomed to sharing. Ultimately though, the joys that effective teaming can yield far outweigh the "jive" we may get along the way. Since it is trying that really counts, give real teaming a try. ▲

The time for going it alone is over.

Interdisciplinary instruction provides many opportunities for one on one conversations.

Worksheet for Use in Planning a Unit

The following is an outline of a process which can be used by teams in planning and implementing an interdisciplinary unit of study.

- TITLE/THEME SELECTED
- SHORT DESCRIPTION/FOCUS OF THE UNIT
- BROAD LEARNING OBJECTIVES TO BE ACHIEVED IN THE UNIT
- IDENTIFY MAJOR IDEAS TO BE STRESSED
- IDENTIFY SKILLS ACROSS THE CONTENT AREAS TO BE TAUGHT
- IDENTIFY MAJOR ATTITUDES TO BE DEVELOPED.
- STRATEGIES/METHODOLOGIES TO BE EMPLOYED:
    1. Direct experiences
    2. Simulations, role-playing/dramatizations and/or debates
    3. Investigations and/or study trips
    4. Constructions (/exhibits, TV programs, murals, interviews, etc.)
    5. Read and/or listen to: (literature, speakers, community resources, etc.)
- GROUPINGS TO BE EMPLOYED: WHICH LEARNING EXPERIENCES ARE MOST EFFECTIVELY PROVIDED IN:
    A. Large group activities?
    B. Small group activities?
    C. Cooperative learning activities?
    D. Individual activities?
- WHAT TYPE OF UNIT EVALUATION COULD OR SHOULD BE USED?
    Post-testing?
    Performance-based assessment?
- TIME-LINE AND RESPONSIBILITY PLAN
    Activity
    When/where
    Who's responsible?
    Deadline?
- ANNOTATED LIST OF RESOURCES AND MATERIALS
- TEAM REFLECTIONS AND EVALUATION OF TEACHING THE UNIT IN ORDER TO IMPROVE THE EFFECTIVESS ON THE NEXT UNIT, AND FOR IMPROVING THIS SPECIFIC UNIT FOR NEXT YEAR. STUDENT EVALUATION OF THE UNIT IS IMPORTANT TO CONSIDER ALSO.

Developed by Sue Swaim, University of Northern Colorado Laboratory School

Webbing: A Format for Planning Integrated Curricula

PHYLLIS SALTZMAN LEVY

A technique that generates ideas and activities and helps to develop long range plans is described by this teacher.

Webbing deserves widespread use as a means of organizing one's thinking about a topic and generates a great variety of possible activities. Webbing is particularly suited for middle school because it can be used to facilitate team planning and integration of content around a specified theme. That is, a math teacher, a language teacher, a social studies teacher, and a science teacher could use a web to plan a unit on 18th century United States. Each would contribute to the formation of the web as described in the balance of this article The result would be that the students would get a sense of wholeness about the theme; and the student would not have to cope with switching on and off her/his mind upon entering and exiting each class during the day.

HOW TO WEB

I. The Question Web

A group of teachers work together to make a web (so-called because the final product looks somewhat like a spider's web).

1) In the center of a large piece of paper, they write the topic. For example, using the topic Chinese Culture:

Moving from the center outwards,

2) several questions might be asked about the topic to begin to form the web.

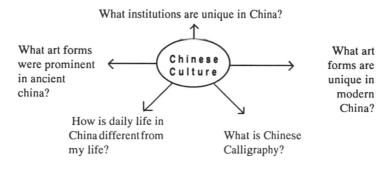

3) Two or three activities are "invented" for each question and recorded. They are worded in a way to indicate action. A good example would be "Students will participate in a learning center which will give them experience in practicing the calligraphy forms." A bad example is "Students learn about calligraphy forms." If additional questions become apparent at this time, add them to the web.

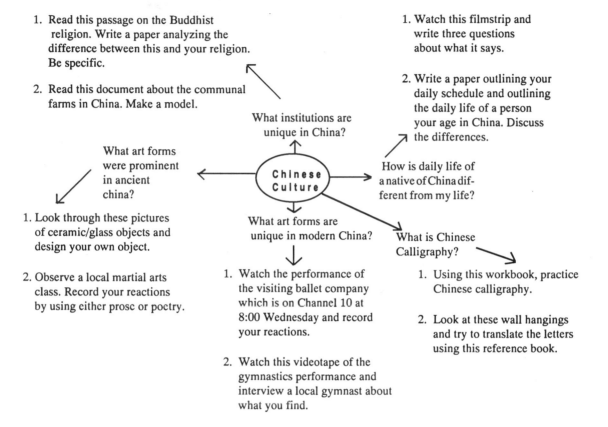

1. Read this passage on the Buddhist religion. Write a paper analyzing the difference between this and your religion. Be specific.

2. Read this document about the communal farms in China. Make a model.

What institutions are unique in China?

1. Watch this filmstrip and write three questions about what it says.

2. Write a paper outlining your daily schedule and outlining the daily life of a person your age in China. Discuss the differences.

What art forms were prominent in ancient china?

Chinese Culture

How is daily life of a native of China different from my life?

1. Look through these pictures of ceramic/glass objects and design your own object.

2. Observe a local martial arts class. Record your reactions by using either prose or poetry.

What art forms are unique in modern China?

What is Chinese Calligraphy?

1. Using this workbook, practice Chinese calligraphy.

2. Look at these wall hangings and try to translate the letters using this reference book.

1. Watch the performance of the visiting ballet company which is on Channel 10 at 8:00 Wednesday and record your reactions.

2. Watch this videotape of the gymnastics performance and interview a local gymnast about what you find.

OTHER WAYS TO WEB

II. The Sub-topic Web

Use of questions to structure a web is only one technique. A second technique is to use subtopics related to the topic. This time, the topic of architecture will be placed in the center of a large piece of paper. Next, subtopics related to the main topic are specified:

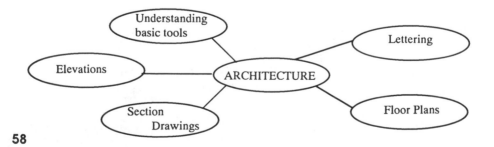

Understanding basic tools

Elevations

Lettering

ARCHITECTURE

Section Drawings

Floor Plans

And finally, two or three activities are created for each subtopic as was done in the case of the Chinese culture questions. Many more components could be used. The components should have some relation to the central topic. Finally, several activities are invented for each component as in the previous illustrations.

III. The Interdisciplinary Web

When an interdisciplinary team is trying to plan a unit together, a more complex form of web might be needed. Instead of the three-steps it takes to create either the question web or the subtopic web, this interdisciplinary web is created in four steps. For example, using the topic of aviation: Moving from the center of the paper outwards, several discipline areas are placed around the topic:

The components of each discipline are identified:

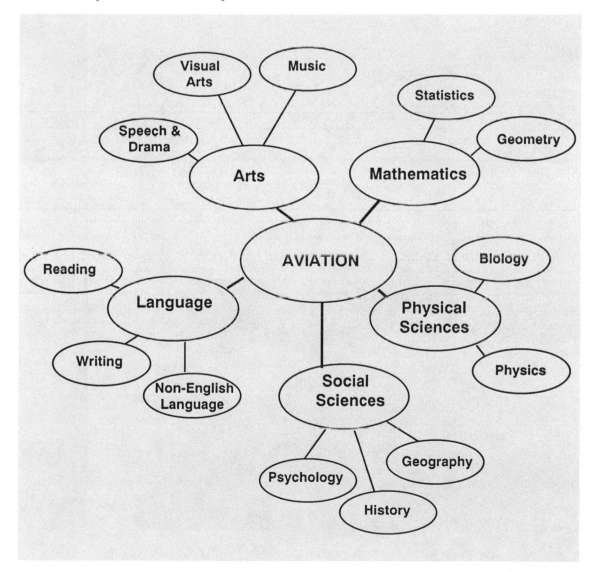

AFTER THE WEB IS COMPLETE

Using the ideas generated by webbing, the teachers then select certain of the activity suggestions and fit them into a linear day-by-day lesson plan form. A variation on this process is to let the students make the selections. Either way, the teacher then knows what is to be accomplished and everyone involved can feel successful when the goal is achieved.

The final product of this procedure might look very much the same as the product of traditional planning. Differences are that the creation of the activities has been done in an organized, careful manner, the activities will reflect greater variety, and the activities assigned by any single student's teachers will have a relation to each other. This qualitative difference is noteworthy, and the difference is clearly in harmony with what middle schools are trying to accomplish. ▲

Common planning time makes the needed collaboration possible.

Planning: The Key To Successful Interdisciplinary Teaching

Shirley F. Heck

Two strategies for planning interdisciplinary units
that involve students are described here by a teacher.

Frequently, interdisciplinary teams fail to realize the instructional and curricular potential of an interdisciplinary unit. Lack of planning skills is a major reason for this condition.

The Role of the Teacher in Planning

Interdisciplinary planning is a very personal matter. The teacher's own experiences, life situations, trips, and cultural activities come into play, These along with magazines and newspaper articles, radio and television programs can be integrated into the lesson plans and shared with students.

The world outside the classroom is a resource for children's learning, so the school experience should go beyond the four walls, both bringing the world into the classroom and taking the class out into the world (Spodek, 1972). The "world around them is an interdisciplinary one." Life is not separated into discrete subject areas. To help teachers plan lessons across various disciplines, several strategies are presented in this article.

The "Lesson Plan Tree": A Strategy to Facilitate Interdisciplinary Planning

The "Lesson Plan Tree" (Cobes & Heck, 1977) is a bulletin board map for planning and implementing interdisciplinary studies. Like any map, it shows both the destination, as well as numerous routes leading to and from this end point. The tree makes the interdisciplinary studies clearer to students. It shows how each topic is graphically related to other topics and to the whole. The Lesson Plan Tree, cut out of construction paper, can be a mere outline of a tree or a realistic representation of a tree pinned to a bulletin board. Roots, trunk, and major branches identify major subject areas of investigation. The class then progressively adds smaller branches and pins on labels and leaves to designate the sub-divisions. Most sub-divisions will represent small group research or experimental activities. Children can either select the activities or cooperatively plan with the teacher which activities they will pursue. Names of children can be placed on leaves and pinned next to the activities they have selected to do.

The tree serves as a motivational device, allowing each class member to understand how his or her contribution relates to the whole. Understanding is facilitated by helping children relate new experiences to those already encountered. The "Lesson Plan Tree" has served as a basis for generating and relating small group interdisciplinary projects, research and problem-solving activities, and role-playing.

61

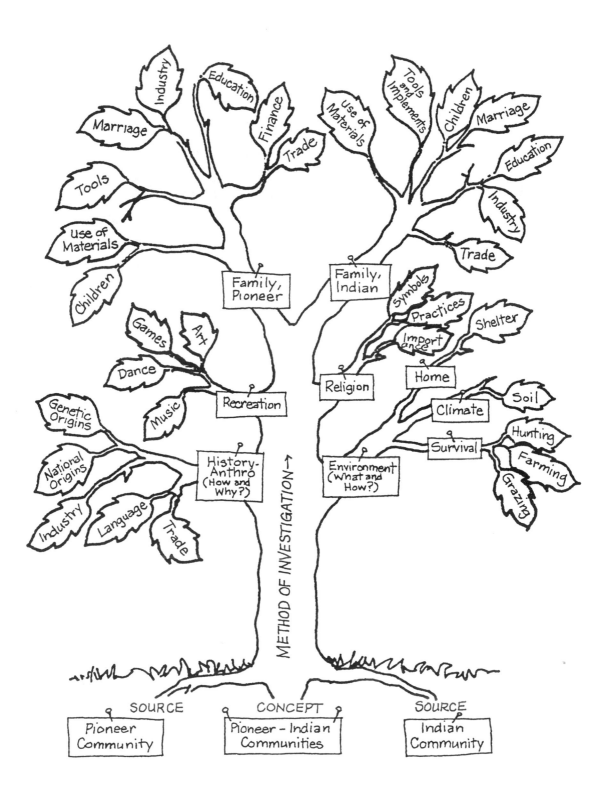

The Lesson Plan Tree

The Lesson Plan Tree illustrates a plan for studying the Pioneer/Indian community. The historical influences on the Indians and the Pioneers, their use of the environment for food, clothing, and shelter, and their ways of satisfying their social, recreational and religious needs are charted graphically on the Lesson Plan Tree. Viewing the tree, one can readily see how the larger problem of contrasting and comparing communal life of the Indians with that of the Pioneers grows out of a complexity of smaller problems.

The Interdisciplinary Planning Wheel

Planning specific interdisciplinary activities can be achieved by use of an Interdisciplinary Planning Wheel. A large wheel can be pinned on a bulletin board, or actually painted on the blackboard. The various social and physical sciences are placed along the circumference of the circle.

Related activities are placed within the appropriate wedges. A plastic acetate sheet can be placed over the wheel and students can write their names in the respective places to identify the activities they are researching.

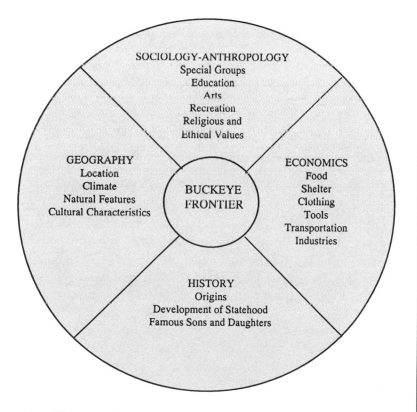

To illustrate the use of the Interdisciplinary Wheel, examples from a unit on the Ohio Frontier follow.

Sample Activities Related to Geography

1. Make maps indicating the land grants, the roads cut into the territory, the location of the Northwestern Territory, and the locations of the early settlements.
2. Collect illustrations of trees, plants, and animals found by the early settlers.

Sample Activities Related to
Sociology - Anthropology

1. Learn typical dances such as the Minuet and the Virginia Reel.
2 Role-play/write a play about frontier life.
3. To help students realize how difficult it was for families to pack up and go west, role play a current family scene in which father comes home and discusses the need to move to another distant state. The reactions of the teenagers, the star football player of the family, the married child, the mother, the grand-parents, might be enacted and discussed.
4. There was little time for recreation in pioneer days, fun was gained primarily through activities related to work. Research ways in which people entertained themselves.

Sample Activities Related to Economics

1. A loom or spinning wheel demonstration by a local craftsperson.
2. After researching the thematic time period, design various types of clothing. Old dyed sheets can be used for special effects in costuming, as well as the use of clothing children already have. Basic clothes can be altered with crepe paper, other material, or paper designs; jewelry, hats, wigs, purses, and scarfs can give a sense of authenticity.
3. Construct a log cabin using rug rolls. Cracks can be chinked with chips and a mixture of clay and moss. Such questions as the following should be researched, discussed, and added to the Kernel Design: How was the interior of the cabin divided? What activities were carried on within the pioneer's cabin that are not common today? Because of housing and living condi-tions, do you think the pioneers thought of themselves as being poor? How did pioneer families manage to survive between the time they arrived in the Ohio country and the time they built their shelters? What kind of furniture did the frontier family have? Was their furniture purchased or made? Were aesthetic qualities important in furnishing a pioneer home? What utensils were commonly found in a pioneer house? What household items were highly valued by the pioneer family?
4. Construct a model of a fort with blockhouses, a covered wagon, and a flatboat.

5. Acquire wool, flax, and cotton from farms if possible. It could be cleaned, carded, dyed, and spun into yarn.
6. Prepare a meal using only foods available to the frontier people.
7. Research ways of food preservation, such as drying, salting, and pickling.
8. Make puppets to illustrate clothing of the period.

Sample Activities Related to Historical Developments
1. Invite the curator from a local museum to speak on artifacts from the area.
2. Have students write imaginative diaries of people who lived during the time of the early settlement. Have children locate copies of original narratives if available in local library.
3. Publish a weekly "Buckeye Frontier Newspaper."
4. Have students write their own genealogies or histories of their national origins.
5. Plan study tours to local historical sites.

Sample Activities Related to Science/Math
1. Research answers to the following questions: How did the pioneers provide light in the cabin? What methods did the pioneer use to clear the land? Who did this work? What tools were used? How did the pioneer pay for outside help?
2. Make dyes from plants in the area.
3. Start small gardens showing the crops that were grown by settlers.

In designing activities related to the various disciplines it is important to consider the types of questions that will stimulate problem-solving processes. Questions should emphasize how and why, instead of what and when. Exploratory questions, such as, "why did the events take place, why do people live and act as they do, and how do conditions and events affect people" can be typed on activity cards for the students to research.

Brainstorming
Basic to the use of both the "Lesson Plan Tree" and the "Interdisciplinary Planning Wheel" is the art of brainstorming. Brainstorming with other teachers and students is one of the best ways to generate many meaningful activities. In working with a group of middle school teachers, the author of this article found it helpful to reprint the experiences which lead to student learning suggested by Brown et al. (1973). Teachers brainstormed activities to correspond with each of the learning behaviors. Often a list of action verbs helps teachers recall more readily potential exploratory activities. The list of learning experiences generated by Brown et al. (1973) includes the following:

It's tough having a team of teachers.

They talk about me. They know my good points and weaknesses, They know if I'm goofing off. Even though they try to help me, I'm not sure I like having four more parents.

- Robert Ricken, *Love Me When I'm Most Unlovable,* Book 2, NASSP.

Thinking	Painting	Viewing
Discussing	Drawing	Exchanging
Reporting	Photographing	Recording
Reading	Working	Taping
Writing	Demonstrating	Dramatizing
Listening	Experimenting	Singing
Interviewing	Problem Solving	Imagining

The following sequence of planning procedures was developed by a group of teachers who have been successful in planning and implementing interdisciplinary units:

1 . At the beginning of the year identify the major units to be developed throughout the year.

2. Have each teacher select one or two units that he/she will be responsible for coordinating.

3. The coordinator assumes leadership responsibility in defining the agenda for the team planning sessions; conducting the brainstorming sessions; assigning group tasks; contacting the appropriate resource people; organizing the classroom environment.

4. As soon as one unit is being implemented, the coordinator assigned for the next unit begins the planning cycle.

Another general suggestion offered by these teachers was to notify and involve the media specialist and/or librarian during the initial planning sessions. These resource people can provide information regarding the availability of relevant films, filmstrips, recordings, simulation kits, primary source material, literature collections, biographies, and community resource people and sites.

When in-depth planning of diversified interdisciplinary activities exist, the classroom becomes a place where students discover the joy of knowledge, the potential of ideas, and the fun of learning. Though the emphasis is on the free experience of discovery and active involvement in the learning process, the classroom activities are planned and structured to make the most of the few short years when young minds are most receptive to ideas and, therefore, to learning. Planning is indeed the key to opening the classroom doors to successful and meaningful learning experiences. The "Lesson Plan Tree" and the "Interdisciplinary Planning Wheel" are offered as strategies to facilitate effective, cooperative planning. ▲

References

Brown, M., Precious, N. *The Integrated Day in the Primary School.* London: Agathon Press, 1968.

Cobes, J., Heck, S.F. "Lesson Plan Tree." *The Science Teacher, Vol. 44, No. 1,* January, 1977.

Fox, James H. "Planning Interdisciplinary Units Within a Team Structure." *Middle School Journal.* Winter, 1974

Spodek, B. *Teaching in the Early Years.* New Jersey; Prentice Hall, Inc., 1972

The Natural for Interdisciplinary Instruction

Toni Worsham

Using thinking skills as the common denominator
for interdisciplinary instruction rather than a theme

There is almost unanimous agreement that an interdisciplinary program is most advantageous for many reasons ranging from increased teacher awareness of student performance to a more coordinated instructional program. The real problem becomes how to develop such a program effectively.

Teachers complain that it is difficult enough to "cover" what must be taught in their own subjects without struggling through long planning sessions with teachers of other disciplines trying to find and develop appropriate interdisciplinary themes and concepts. Frustration and disappointment often follow long hours of team planning because the themes are difficult to discover and to develop and the resulting units are frequently artificial and inappropriate to one or more of the disciplines. Only by "stretching the imagination" and pulling the curriculum in unusual and unnatural directions can it be made to "fit" the interdisciplinary themes.

Several questions arise when teachers, in the name of interdisciplinary instruction, are made to work through such time-consuming and generally disappointing experiences. Is it all worth it? Is there an easier way? Is there really a natural basis for interdisciplinary program planning and instruction?

The answer to all these questions is an emphatic "yes"! Moreover, like so many answers to problems long pondered, the solution is really rather simple although obviously not immediately realized. A few more questions need to be considered before the "answer" and a successful application of its effectiveness is shared.

Is there a common denominator for learning? Is it vital to all curricula? Is its basis universal? Can it be taught more effectively via an interdisciplinary approach? Does it occur naturally within any existing content? The answer to each question once again is "yes."

The common denominator is the thinking process. It is absolutely essential for successful learning and best learned via an interdisciplinary approach which allows students to readily see that thinking skills learned in one class are generally transferable and useful in attaining objectives requiring similar problem-solving thought processes in other classes.

How does a team of teachers begin to develop an interdisciplinary program using thinking skills (rather than content, concepts, or themes) as the basis for team planning? The sixth grade teacher team at Patapsco Middle

School in Howard County, Maryland found an effective way. By following those steps required to implement the "Inclusion Process," a direct instructional model for teaching thinking, the team found not only an excellent approach to thinking skills instruction but a basis for interdisciplinary planning that was natural for four content areas (language arts, math, social studies, and science) and useful to each teacher in helping students to learn the content of their respective disciplines.

The "Inclusion Process" model, developed by the author over a period of two years, is based primarily on the results of research showing the positive effect of thinking skills instruction on verbal SAT scores (Worsham and Austin, 1983) and careful analysis of those characteristics common to many commercially developed thinking skills programs. The process consists of eight steps listed on the left column which can be applied at any educational level and in any and all content areas. Currently, schools in four Maryland counties are using the model.

Implementation Procedures

The Maryland State Department of Education awarded a grant to Howard County which enabled the Patapsco team to implement a pilot project during the 1984-85 school year according to the following procedures:

—Each of the four teachers independently listed those thinking skills which seemed to be essential to learning their respective subjects. (Step 1)

—Each teacher then reduced the list to five skills which students did not apply effectively. (Step 2)

—The teachers then met as an interdisciplinary team to share their lists and reach consensus regarding which skills they would teach via direct instruction. (Step 3)

The four skills selected were:

• Understanding the main idea

• Reading charts, graphs, and cartoons

• Recognizing logical relationships

• Predicting outcomes

—The team then determined the sequence for teaching the skills and who would be responsible for teaching the Focus Lesson (the 2-3 period lesson during which step 5, defining the skill, and 6, listing the steps necessary to apply the skill) for each skill. It was decided that each teacher would be responsible for teaching one of the four Focus lessons according to the following sequence

English—Understanding the main idea

Social Studies—Reading charts, graphs, and cartoons

Math—Recognizing logical relationships

Science—Predicting outcomes

— Before the Focus Lessons were actually taught to the students, the teacher team went through the process of defining the skills and listing the steps for each of the four skills themselves. This not only provided them with an agreed upon definition and procedure for application of each skill but enabled the teachers to anticipate some of the difficulties that students might encounter as they tried to generate their own definitions and sequencing of steps. (Steps 5 and 6)

The teachers defined "understanding the main idea" as follows:

"Understanding the main idea means finding and stating in your own words the most important point."

Their steps were:
1. Examine the material presented
2. Pick out key parts (words, phrases, ideas, concepts)
3. Select supporting details
4. Discard unimportant material
5. Analyze what is left
6. State the most important point m your own words
7. Test the strength of the stated main idea.
8. Revise the statement (if necessary).

Also, each teacher taught the planned Focus Lesson to the other teachers prior to actually teaching the lesson to the students. This allowed any necessary adjustments to be made and increased the effectiveness of each lesson.

The Focus Lessons were most crucial in ensuring that students would successfully learn each of the four skills. The common denominator was that students generate and reach class consensus regarding both the definition and the steps necessary to apply each skill.

Each teacher taught the Focus Lesson to the other teachers prior to teaching it to students.

Examples

The following are some examples of the definitions and steps students generated:

UNDERSTANDING THE MAIN IDEA

DEFINITION
Understanding the main idea is knowing the most important thought and expressing it in your own words.

STEPS
1. Examine the material
2. Sort out important parts/details
3. Leave out unimportant parts
4. Study what is left
5. Express the main idea in your own words
6. Make necessary changes
7. Test your statement

MAKING A PREDICTION

DEFINITION
Making a prediction is using what you already know (facts, theories) and your imagination to make an educated guess about what could happen in the future.

STEPS
1. Gather information
2. Sort out information to find what you need.
3. Put information together to make a prediction sentence.
4. Review information.
5. Add or take away what you need or don't need. ,
6. Improve prediction.
7. Try other possibilities.

—Following completion of the Focus Lesson each teacher agreed to include at least two activities related to the subject which required students to apply the recently learned thinking skill (Step 7). These activities ranged from 10 or 15 minutes to full period application lessons.

Students were instructed to designate a section of their notebook for "Thinking Skills."

The definitions and steps were kept in this section. Students quickly recognized that the thinking skills learned in one class were useful in completing objectives in their other classes as well! The following is a sample application activity:

Students quickly recognized that the thinking skills learned in one class were useful in completing objectives in other classes.

Sample Application Lesson

Thinking Skill: Finding the main idea
Subject Area: Any
Suggested Level: Elementary or middle school
Objectives: To find the main idea in a short written paragraph by differentiating between supporting statements and the central focus of the passage.
Materials: Worksheet (included), chalkboard or overhead, short paragraphs taken from appropriate printed materials and mounted on construction paper.

Procedures:

1. Explain to the class that the main idea of a paragraph is like an umbrella that covers all the ideas in the paragraph. Show an illustration.

2. Have students work in small groups. Provide several examples of paragraphs. Number each to avoid confusion. Students will read three short paragraphs and record the main idea and the supporting details on the umbrella illustrations.

3. Remove the titles and subtitles from the paragraphs to make the work more challenging.

4. Allow a 10-15 minute work period and then ask each group to share its umbrella diagrams with the class

Evaluation/follow-up: Ask students to find a paragraph in a newspaper or a magazine and diagram the main idea and supporting ideas on the umbrella model .

(Developed by Bill Hodge, Science and Language Arts teacher, Thurmont Middle School, Frederick, MD. Used with permission.)

Main Idea and Supporting Details

Directions:

1. Work with your group on one paragraph at a time.

2. Read each paragraph silently and aloud.

3. Discuss the main idea of the paragraph and the supporting ideas.

4. Choose a recorder to write your thoughts down on scrap paper.

5. When the group is satisfied that you have found the main idea and the supporting details, write the paragraph number above the umbrella on the diagram and the supporting ideas underneath the umbrella on the lines provided.

6. Write the main idea on the top portion of the umbrella.

Finally, the teachers included both questions on knowledge and application of the skill on their tests (Step 8). This helped students understand that the thinking skills which they were learning were as much a part of their program as the content matter of the various disciplines.

Additional opportunities were provided for students to apply their thinking skills over the summer months in "think logs." These "logs" required students to write about one (1) life situation per week in which they were able to apply one of the four skills they had learned.

The teachers met on five Saturdays during the year to develop and critique lessons, discuss problems, and exchange ideas regarding their interdisciplinary model. Also, several inservice workshops were

Teachers included questions on knowledge about and application of skills on their tests.

Students applied their thinking skills over the summer months in "think logs."

provided on such topics as brainstorming, concept attainment, "Think-pair-share (Lyman, 1981), grouping, and modeling to give teachers diverse instructional strategies useful in implementing the "Inclusion Process" model .

Both teachers and students responded enthusiastically to the thinking skills interdisciplinary model. The math teacher noted that via the skill planning periods she always knew what was going on in the other classes and was often able to refer to or build upon her colleagues' units in math. The English language arts teacher, who was also the team leader, noted that it was the best interdisciplinary approach she had ever used and that the teachers had really functioned as a "team" by using this approach. Students said they liked hearing their teachers refer to work they had done in their other classes.

A $5,000 grant was awarded to Howard County by the state to continue this project in 1985-86. Plans included using the money to extend the model to the seventh grade. The teachers selected four or five additional skills to teach while also reviewing the four skills taught in the sixth grade. During the third year the process was repeated in the 8th grade.

By the end of the eighth grade the students had learned about a dozen thinking skills via this interdisciplinary model. Additionally, a curriculum activity packet containing the focus lessons and numerous follow-up activities used by the teachers for each skill was made available to other county schools.

Finally, the students were tested via a county-made test to determine the extent to which they had learned the selected thinking skills.

Research shows that less than 40% of high school graduates are able to reason effectively (Day, 1981). These students entered high school better equipped to handle higher-order thinking tasks.

Enthusiasm was high among students, teachers, administrators, and central office staff regarding the model. Students indicated in a county-administered questionnaire that they were pleased that their teachers were planning and teaching thinking skills together. They also felt that what they were learning in thinking was important both in and out of school.

Most importantly, the thinking skills approach provided teachers and students with a natural basis for interdisciplinary planning, teaching, and learning. ▲

REFERENCES

Day, M.C. "Thinking at Piaget's Stage of Formal Operations." *Educational Leadership,* October 1981, pp. 44 47.

Lyman, F.T. "The Responsive Classroom Discussion: The Inclusion of ALL Students." *Mainstreaming Digest,* A.S. Anderson, (Ed.), 1981: University of Maryland, College Park, Maryland

Worsham, A.M. & Austin, G.R. "Effects of Teaching Thinking Skills on SAT Scores." *Educational Leadership.* November 1983, pp. 50-51.

Cross-Curricular Connections

JOAN MAUTE

Opportunities abound to correlate and integrate separate subjects.
The author presents a way of looking at these "connections."

One of the great advantages of interdisciplinary teaming is the opportunity it gives teachers to integrate learning among various subjects. This intertwining of subject matter not only reinforces what is taught, but also more closely resembles life outside the classroom where the subjects we teach are not found in isolation, but, rather, are constantly interacting with and overlapping each other. As a teacher in a school that made the transition from a departmentalized structure to one with interdisciplinary teams, I found that we were constantly being bombarded with information about something called ''I.D.U.'' Once we realized that this was *not* a form of birth control but an Interdisciplinary Unit, we were excited about creating and implementing our own I.D.U.'s — and became believers.

Teams at our school engage in many I.D.U.'s each year, and they never fail to get students involved with and enthusiastic about the topic. Because of the success of these units I believe we need to look more closely for other ways to integrate learning. Perhaps we should put less emphasis on occasional large units and more emphasis on the day-to-day potential that exists for cross-curricular connections. Cross-curricular connections are connections between two or more areas of study that are made by teachers within the structure of their disciplines. Examples could include music and math; art and advisory; English, science, and physical education; and so on. One might think of the middle school curriculum as a pinball machine with the subjects being the bumpers and the teacher being the ball that can help the player (student) win by making connections.

But Why Bother?

There are many reasons to use cross-curricular connections. These connections can help us reach students with various learning styles. By using art or music in any of the basic subjects a teacher can appeal to visual and auditory learners. The kinetic learning inherent in classes such as industrial arts and home economics does not have to be limited to just those courses. Food from various countries can be served in a world cultures class, and instruments made in shop can be played in music. Utilizing cross-curricular connections also allows for capitalizing on students' subject preferences. Most students prefer one or more subjects over others; by making cross-curricular connections, the student who dislikes math may find it more palatable when it is applied in a favorite social studies or English class.

Students can apply what is learned in one area to another area of study much more readily when teachers make cross-curricular connections. Such applications give learning greater meaning as the original learning is reinforced and the new learning becomes more familiar. In some cases cross-curricular connections can help bridge the gap between theory and practice. Through seeing cross-curricular relationships, students can begin to realize that learning, like life, is not a spectator sport.

Maute's Hierarchy of Cross-Curricular Connections

As you might guess, there are many levels and examples of cross-curricular connections. At the base of this hierarchy is what I like to call the *cross-curricular incident*. The incident can happen more frequently than other types of connections. It is very simple and, once mastered, becomes so natural that students and teachers take it for granted. An incident happens when a social studies teacher, who knows the English teacher is teaching adjectives, asks the students for adjectives to describe a country, civilization, landform, or event. Incidents occur when math teachers compare fractions to music notes or when art teachers talk of proportions used to mix colors. You can see how the list of incidents could go on forever, and right now I'm sure you can think of cross-curricular incidents that are happening or could be happening all the time in your subject.

> **Perhaps we should put less emphasis on occasional large units and more emphasis on the day-to-day potential that exists for cross-curricular connections.**

> **Through seeing cross-curricular relationships, students can begin to realize that learning, like life, is not a spectator sport.**

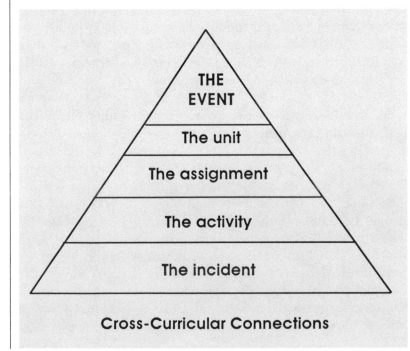

THE
EVENT

The unit

The assignment

The activity

The incident

Cross-Curricular Connections

The next step up from the incident is the *cross-curricular activity*. I play a game in sixth-grade social studies called Silent World. This game is a modification of that elementary favorite, Silent Ball. In Silent World students sit on their desks and gently (I always remind them to be gentle with our world) toss an inflatable globe from student to student. The room is completely silent except when a student catches the world. When the student catches the world, he or she must tell the class what continent or ocean his or her right thumb is on or closest to. I have one globe that also has animals placed on their home continent or ocean. In that game students name the animal as well as the continent or ocean. If they miss the world or talk out of turn, they become a spectator, not participants in the game. This activity incorporates reading, social studies, science, and physical education as the students become aware of the relative locations of oceans, continents, and animals while practicing the study skills of listening and following directions.

Music can be used to introduce lessons in social studies (Maute, 1988). Any activity that happens within a class and incorporates two or more subject areas can be classified as a cross-curricular activity. As you think through the last unit you taught you will become aware of the fact that you had some cross-curricular activities. Now think of more you could add as you continue through your present unit.

As we work our way up the hierarchy, we now encounter the *cross-curricular assignment*. This assignment requires the student to do work, either in or out of class, that involves two or more disciplines. When my students were reading *The Phantom Tollbooth, I* copied the map from the inside cover of the book. I drew longitude and latitude lines on the map and asked my students to list the coordinates for Dictionopolis, Digitopolis, the Tollbooth, the Doldrums, and other locations in the story. The math teacher expanded the assignment by asking the students to create a scale and measure distances between points on the map. These assignments allowed us to reinforce earlier learnings in our subjects while giving the students a fuller understanding of the land about which they were reading.

When given a choice, students often make their own cross-curricular connections using their preferred learning modes. Illustrations can become concrete ways of learning idioms while students practice art in English. Writing and performing a "rap" song (Maute, 1987) can help students remember facts as they lead the rest of the class in review. Concrete learners can build models for science or social studies to show what they have learned. The cross-curricular assignment is very likely already present in many of your school's classes.

It is not unusual for a team to suspend "regular" classes while implementing an interdisciplinary unit.

Students often make their own cross-curricular connections using their preferred learning modes.

We have now worked our way up to the I.D.U., *Interdisciplinary Units* which combine incidents, activities, and assignments. They frequently provide short term, in-depth focus on a specific topic (Kerekes, 1987). It is not unusual for a team to suspend "regular" classes while implementing an interdisciplinary unit. Well-received interdisciplinary units require a lot of planning, energy, and creativity. They provide a break from the usual routine and are thoroughly enjoyed by students and teachers alike. The value of a good interdisciplinary unit cannot be overemphasized.

At the top of the hierarchy beyond the I.D.U., we find the ultimate cross-curricular connection. This is the *cross-curricular EVENT*. Quite often interdisciplinary units will have a culminating event. Our sixth-grade teams finish their interdisciplinary unit on Greece and Rome with the Greek and Roman Festival. Over the years we have included food prepared by the students, a catapult contest, banners, Olympic events, newspapers, drama, "Meet Our City-state" television programs (Athens A.M. or Troy Today complete with the latest traffic and weather reports), gods and goddesses, and every student in a costume as part of the festival. Students remember these events forever (Who could forget the sight of 150 sixth graders in sheets?), but the incidents, activities, assignments, and units make the events possible.

Putting It Together

There are three major pieces to the cross-curricular puzzle. The first and most important piece is awareness of what is being taught in other classes. Any connection between subject areas is good, but, if connections are made parallel to each other, they are even better. You cannot make connections with what is going on currently in another class if you do not know what is being taught there. For interdisciplinary teams this information comes in a team meeting. Our team committed one meeting a week for "academic plans." We used this time to schedule tests for the following week and let each other know what we were teaching in both the near and distant future. As time went on, we became more aware of each other's curricula and could work toward more correlation. It is more difficult to become aware of the content being taught outside of your team, so some forum should exist to accomplish this. What your students learn in physical education, music art, shop, home economics, computers, foreign language, and other exploratories especially needs to be connected with the basic subjects.

The second piece of the good cross-curricular puzzle is planning. Once you are aware of curriculum outside of your own, you can work alone or with other teachers to look for connections, and plan incidents, activities, assignments, units, and events that take advan-

You cannot make connections with what is going on in another class if you don't know what is being taught there.

Our team committed one meeting a week for "academic plans."

tage of this knowledge. The higher up the pyramid you go, the more planning becomes necessary.

The final piece to the puzzle is flexibility. Once you have achieved awareness and planning, you must be willing to fold, bend, stretch, move, and, yes, even sometimes leave out part of what you had planned. The results will be more responsive to your students' needs and have more meaning as new and old learnings in many areas become fused . As you continue to work with these and look for connections, you will see your students beginning to make connections on their own.

Returning to the pinball machine analogy, the more frequently the ball bounces off various bumpers, the higher the score will be. The ball can travel from bumper to bumper for quite a while on its own but not forever. To truly win the game, it becomes necessary for the player to hit the flippers and try to make more connections. True interdisciplinary teaching is ongoing. As teachers we should be striving not only to make connections for our students, but also to teach them to see and make their own connections. When they have connected with learning, applied it in many areas, and revised and revamped their knowledge, they can't help being winners.

References

Kerekes, J. (1987, August) The interdisciplinary unit . . . it's here to stay! *Middle School Journal*, pp. 12-14.

Maute, J. (1988, January) Rapping and mapping. *Science Scope*, pp. 44-45.

Maute, J. (1987, February) Tune in memory. *Middle School Journal*, pp. 3-5.

Post Script   July 1992

When I wrote "Cross-Curricular Connections" I was in my third year of teaming and my first year as a member of the "Encore" (exploratory, allied arts) Team at Hill Middle School. As I have continued to work with students and teachers it has become very clear that the article needs to be expanded.

The question "What *is* curriculum?" needs to be reexamined. As the view of curriculum broadens, so do the possibilities for connections. I like to think of curriculum as a camera with a zoom lens. Sometimes the lens is on a macro setting and only focussing on a very small part of the whole, but at other times wide-angle and telephoto settings reveal new parts and content for the middle school curriculum. Curriculum therefore is not limited to what is planned for our classrooms, or even to what takes place in classrooms, but must include all facets of the culture and activities of our schools. There is curriculum in the lunchroom, the hallways, the busses, as well as in activities, events, relationships, and classes. Traditionally it is the teacher who is aiming the lens and therefore controlling what the curriculum sees. We must remember, however, that our students bring with them their own curriculum and our lens must begin by "seeing" that curriculum and ultimately letting the student become the photographer.

Once the definition of curriculum has been expanded, it is easy to realize that cross-curricular connections can be much more than "connections between two or more areas of study that are made by teachers within the structure of their disciplines." Cross-curricular connections can be connections between any parts of the formal or informal curriculum that are made at any time, by adults and/or students engaged in part of the curriculum in and about school. When the student can not only see the connections but take part in creating the pictures we all can get a clearer view. ▲

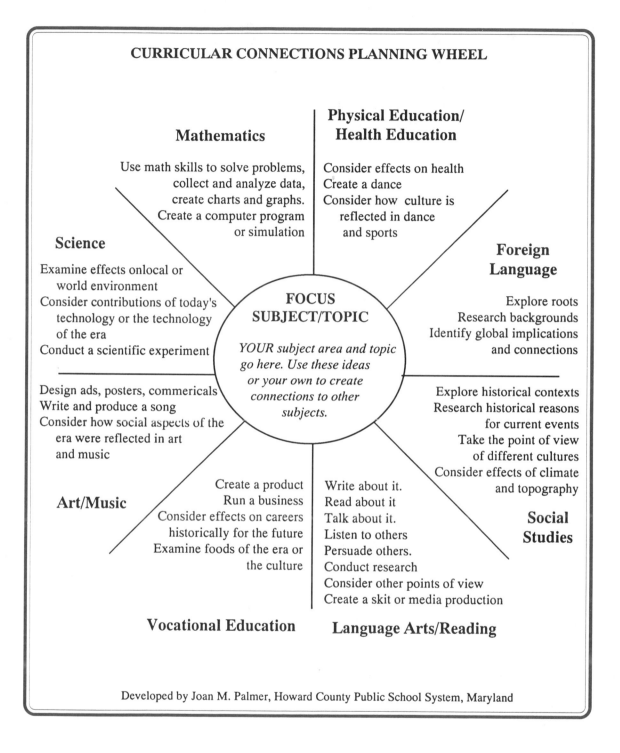

CURRICULAR CONNECTIONS PLANNING WHEEL

Mathematics

Use math skills to solve problems, collect and analyze data, create charts and graphs. Create a computer program or simulation

Physical Education/ Health Education

Consider effects on health
Create a dance
Consider how culture is reflected in dance and sports

Science

Examine effects onlocal or world environment
Consider contributions of today's technology or the technology of the era
Conduct a scientific experiment

Foreign Language

Explore roots
Research backgrounds
Identify global implications and connections

FOCUS SUBJECT/TOPIC

YOUR subject area and topic go here. Use these ideas or your own to create connections to other subjects.

Design ads, posters, commericals
Write and produce a song
Consider how social aspects of the era were reflected in art and music

Explore historical contexts
Research historical reasons for current events
Take the point of view of different cultures
Consider effects of climate and topography

Art/Music

Create a product
Run a business
Consider effects on careers historically for the future
Examine foods of the era or the culture

Write about it.
Read about it
Talk about it.
Listen to others
Persuade others.
Conduct research
Consider other points of view
Create a skit or media production

Social Studies

Vocational Education

Language Arts/Reading

Developed by Joan M. Palmer, Howard County Public School System, Maryland

No matter what the content we can design active linkages between fields of knowledge.
— Heidi Jacobs

SECTION III

Interdisciplinary Instruction in Action

Doda **Nancy Doda,** Educational Consultant, Burke, VA

Haschak **John W. Haschak,** Superintendent of Schools, Greensburg, OH

Buckingham **Francine Buckingham,** Middle School Teacher, Dublin, OH
Jordan **Lucille Jordan,** Middle School Teacher, Dublin, OH
Spangler **Shirley Spangler,** Symphony Orchestra Manager, Anchorage, AK, formerly Middle School Teacher, Dublin, OH

Kerekes **Joanne Kerekes,** Staff Development Coordinator, South Brunswick, NJ School District

Stromberg **Robert B. Stromberg,** Principal, North Attleboro Junior High School, North Attleboro, MA
Smith **Joan M. Smith,** Sixth Grade Teacher, Galvin Middle School, Canton, MA

Daniels **Timothy Daniels,** Superintendent, Octorara Area School District, Atglen, PA
O'Brien **Joseph O'Brien,** Principal, Springfield High School, Springfield, PA
Pittman **Robert Pittman,** Principal, Paxon Hollow Middle School, Marple Newtown, PA

Brodsky **Melvin A. Brodsky,** Principal, Beverly Hills Middle School, Upper Darby, PA

Carr **John Carr,** Associate Professor of Education, Plymouth State College, Plymouth, NH
Eppig **Peter Eppig,** Director, Critical Thinking Skills Program, Antioch New England Graduate School, Keene, NH
Monether **Peter Monether,** Teacher, Great Brook Middle School (formerly Peterborough Middle School), Peterborough, NH

Springer **Mark Springer,** Teacher, Radnor Middle School, Wayne, PA

Two Novices Find Success

Nancy Doda

Learning centers were created for a six week unit to utilize resources and to accommodate varied student schedules.

I. Cooperative Teaching, A Second Look

It's exciting to watch as middle schools across the country bring students and teachers together into smaller, more personal communities for teaching and learning. It's a little discouraging to note, however, that while groups of teachers and students are indeed being transformed into clearly defined and interpersonally involved communities, participation in authentic team teaching is not a simultaneously occurring phenomenon. Why not?

Many middle schools have the conditions necessary for teaming. Teachers and students have a common identity, share a part of the campus, and follow a common schedule. Unfortunately, these same middle schools are often unable to provide teachers with the supportive props which facilitate successful teamed instruction, such as a common planning period, connective classrooms, a flexible block schedule and training in those special skills of team planning and team teaching. As a result, teaming teachers may work hard to create close-knit learning communities but withdraw from invitations to team teach. So it is that teamed teachers often share little more than the same kids, reserving the sharing of lesson plans, teaching talents, and subject area expertise for teaching conditions more suitable.

In a personal effort to promote and preserve team teaching as a viable instructional tool for middle school teachers. I would like to offer an illustration of how two teachers participated in cooperative teaching even without the props. I hope that the description of a real case as well as my analysis will offer impetus and insight to teachers eager to team teach.

II. The Raw Facts

For most of a school year I taught Reading to about 150 students on a team. As one of four team members I shared the same group of students, the same basic schedule, the same hallway, but never the same lesson plans. With lots of students reading below grade level, I found the constant challenge of making reading instruction life-related, difficult and demanding. Moreover, I became concerned about the artificial separation of language arts and reading and its obvious message to the kids. Fortunately, the Language Arts teacher on my team shared these same concerns and so we decided to open our doors to an experiment in cooperative teaching.

Before embarking on this exciting endeavor, we carefully examined our possibilities and limitations. Logistically, cooperative teaching was possible since during four forty-two minute class periods we both taught either Language Arts or Reading to various class combinations of the same students. Our classrooms were connected by a once-blocked doorway so that we could work together with collected groups of sixty students thereby increasing our teaching possibilities.

Several limiting factors had to be considered. Since students on the team followed varying schedules according to their ability group placement in Reading and Math, our combined group of sixty had to be totally regrouped according to our instructional plan. This regrouping had to elicit the necessary changes without disturbing the basic team schedule. For example, every forty-two minutes our students changed classes. This was one variable we could not change. Some students because of their particular class schedule stayed with us for two consecutive periods while others came for one period, left and returned at a later time. Within this framework we designed and executed a teamed unit.

III. "Man In Flight": A Joint Effort
This interdisciplinary unit was created in stages. A brief description of each stage should provide a step-by-step guide for teachers planning such a unit.

STAGE 1—What to Teach?

After brainstorming for several weeks, we compiled a list of learning objectives in Language Arts and Reading. The objectives touched on letter writing, job application, reading comprehension, vocabulary development, following directions, creative writing, and outlining. Since our students had repeatedly expressed an interest in airplanes, flying, and flight, we decided to teach these skills through a thematic unit called, "Man In Flight." Clearly, this theme had possibilities for literature, writing, vocabulary, history, science, math, and a whole wealth of communication skills.

STAGE 2—Gathering Resources

Gathering resources was more stimulating and efficient when we worked together. We were amazed at the resources we were able to tap. Some examples included: local travel agents, airlines, the local airport, NASA, the U.S. Air Force, pilots, and other flight specialists in our community. In addition, all reading textbooks were scoured for flight-related stories and classified according to determined readability levels. Too, our school library supplied books and media related to our unit's theme.

I became concerned about the artificial separation of language arts and reading and its obvious message to the kids.

Gathering resources was more stimulating and efficient when working together.

STAGE 3—Designing Learning Activities

In order to fully utilize all of our resources we decided to use a centers approach individualizing our learning activities according to reading levels, specified by a color coding system. The unit had ten learning stations and one learning packet for all students to experience. Activities in each of the stations varied according to levels with some opportunity for variety according to student interest or learning style.

Six of the centers were set up in one classroom and the remaining were set up in the other. The centers varied according to the skill objectives and two were open-ended. As an example, the center which dealt with following directions was called "Fly Your Own Thing." Students were to build whirly birds, pinwheels, and paper airplanes. Some students constructed model airplanes. Following directions was critical to success, and success was evaluated in our paper airplane flying contest that was held periodically throughout the unit.

STAGE 4—Setting Up

Before the unit could begin, we had to pave the road to its success. Many centers had activities which required students to preview filmstrips or listen to tapes. Accordingly, we built two previewing corners equipped with headphones, tape recorders, and filmstrip previewers. An additional preventive provision was aimed at record-keeping and evaluation. Each student was given one folder for the unit with a special checklist of all the center activities. All work completed would be kept in these folders and each of us would evaluate work done on those centers we specifically designed. For special student cases, we deleted certain centers or included other options not generally available. These would be noted at the bottom of a student's checklist. We kept these folders in two large boxes so that A-M were in one classroom and the remaining N-Z were in the other. Finally, we agreed upon certain guidelines for student behavior and teacher behavior during the unit.

STAGE 5—Orientation

We devoted two full days to orientation. Students were introduced to the centers, and the logistics of our unit. Behavior standards were explored, agreed upon, and established .

STAGE 6—Blast *Off!*

The unit lasted for six weeks. Each week there was a combination of individual work time, small group time, and large group time.

The unit had ten learning stations and one learning packet for all students to experience.

Each student was given one folder for the unit with a special checklist of all the center activities.

Throughout the six weeks, situational meetings were necessary. At one point we found it necessary to make a motivational chart for the drifters who couldn't get started. This was a visible chart for students to refer to regarding their progress. We also designated peer-teaching pairs to help those needing more structure than the unit provided.

IV. What We Discovered

In spite of the frustrations along the way, the unit's success was overwhelming. We happily discovered:

1. Students who were turned off to Language Arts and Reading were newly motivated and worked enthusiastically.

2. Students engaged in self-initiated projects related to but not required by the unit's activities (i.e. a small group designed and built an airport for the future.)

Eleven positive discoveries grew out of the unit's success.

3. Students acknowledged the application of skills to practical situations, (i.e. the need to read directions carefully before filling out a job application).

4. As a result of increased student interest, all but a few students received higher grades. They were pleased with their success.

5. Teaching became more exciting as we shared our successes and failures with each other. The experience encouraged each of us to examine our own teaching strengths and weaknesses.

6. The nature of the unit allowed for student freedom but fostered student self-discipline.

7. With two of us at work, student needs were met more effectively. One could work with a small group while the other facilitated those working individually.

8. The unit involved the math and science teachers on our team. They enriched the unit as visiting instructors and taught related large group lessons.

9. Those skills selected to be taught were successfully mastered as indicated by a final post-test evaluation.

10. Students learned to work together democratically and were pleased to see their teachers cooperating for their welfare.

11. Students were able to work continuously on one integrated learning experience and felt they accomplished more as a result.

Team teaching can bring new life and vitality into your teaching. If you feel courageous here is a final list of helpful suggestions:

1. Start small. Perhaps two team members can experiment before all four members become involved.

2. Assess your logistical limitations. Be realistic.

3. Select a theme according to student interests.

4. Work out roles and personal expectations before you start.

5. Hold frequent problem-solving meetings during the unit.

6. Evaluate your product. Get student feedback.

7. Don't give up.

Though my account is just one example, I hope you are inspired to reconsider cooperative teaching as a valuable instructional tool. Perhaps our individual teaching efforts will draw support so that all middle school students may someday have the exciting kind of learning experience offered through team teaching. ▲

Small groups pursuing special sub-topics are a part of most interdisciplinary units.

Roles and Functions of Team Members

FACILITATOR

Preside over meetings
- arrange agenda, move meeting forward — keep people on task
- bring up and review old business (make sure it gets done)
- liaison between team and other staff

Conflicts between team members
- approaches members in conflict and suggests mediator and if necessary will assist in setting up.
- if conflict includes facilitator, time keeper would take on this responsibility
- coordinates resource people (team inservice)
- facilitate correlation of subjects — tie in topics between classes

CURRICULUM COORDINATOR

Keeps calendar of tests, curriculum and weekly topic agenda for each discipline represented on a team

NOTETAKER/ RECORDER

Keeps written record of team planning topics, decisions, agendas
Make copies for all team members

TIME KEEPER

Alert team to stay on topic
Alert team to the time remaining 5 minutes before end of period
Evaluate meetings a few minutes before end

LIBRARIAN

Keep copies of progress reports for each student
Keep files and team notebook in central location for team
Responsible for team resource material like award certificates, etc.

TREASURER

Keep accurate account of monies belonging to team
In charge of fund raising

FIELD TRIP COORDINATOR

Coordinate field trips among own and other teams
Research possible places for field trips for your team

"P.R." PERSON

In charge of newspaper/newsletter articles for team
In charge of bulletin boards for team (hallways only)
Contact person for media

SPECIAL EVENT COORDINATOR

Arbor Day, MLK Birthday, etc.
Award ceremonies, special speakers for team, etc.

It Happens in the Huddle

JOHN W. HASCHAK

Effective use of common planning time was the key
to the successful implementation of interdisciplinary teaming.

With an all-out effort to better meet the needs of kids and capitalize on staff strengths, the Kimpton Middle School in Stow, Ohio, fully implemented interdisciplinary teaming. The teaming approach represents a complete departure from the previous departmentalized framework. The team structure divides the total 7th and 8th grade student population of 1110 students into nine instructionally independent units of 135 to 158 students. Complete academic organizational responsibility rests in the hands of the five 8th and six 7th grade teachers who comprise the team nuclei. As teamwork is the key to success in athletics, it seems to have provided the catalyst for cooperation and coordination in the interdisciplinary teaming.

Team Personnel

"First string offense" is composed of a language arts, social studies, mathematics, science, and, at the seventh grade, reading instructor. Going both ways and serving on three units, is a team guidance counselor; while the assistant principal and principal tend to function as "defensive specialists" and "general managers." Special personnel called on as needed include the school nurse, school psychologist, curriculum director, creative arts teachers, and career education personnel. Rotating team aides (paraprofessionals previously used to supervise study halls), one per grade level, assist as "front office" personnel of sorts, as they now help with clerical and student supervisory needs.

Schedule

Each team must schedule around the designated times for lunch, physical education, creative arts, and home room. However, the remaining part of the day, referred to as academic time, is the total responsibility of the team. Student schedules, therefore, may be flexibly adjusted to meet varying academic time requirements. A good example would be the team creation of two hours of laboratory time to enable their science instructor to handle the unit on frog dissection, or the elimination of all academics the last period of the day in order to permit a total team recreational or social activity. At selected times, such as when half the students are at physical education, band, or chorus, the remaining members participate in I.G.I. (Individual and Group Instruction), where they may receive academic or social assistance in small groups.

The last period of each day, referred to on the example schedule below as Rotating Reinforcement simply means the students will have two sessions of a given subject on a particular day. This team uses four days of R. R. with Wednesday's 8th period being used for Individual and Group Instruction again.

8:10	9:00	9:50	10:40	11:25-55	12:47	1:30	2:00	3:30
I.G.I. of Spelling P.E.	Academic	I.G.I. of Chorus (tutoring)	Academic	Lunch	Academic	Academic	Creative Arts HUDDLE (team planning)	Rotating Reinforcement I.G.I. Wed. (values clarification activity)

The Huddle

We are finding that the greatest benefits are coming from "the huddle" or daily team planning period. While students are attending their creative arts selection (i.e., their electives which include sewing, cooking, making music, sound lab, crafts, drawing, metals, or woods), their teaching team, including a counselor, is involved in a fifty minute planning period we call "the huddle."

The huddle remains open, with the designated team leader calling the plays and each team member having an opportunity to contribute as often as desired. The unlabeled circle in the diagram may be filled by any of the specialty personnel listed to provide assistance as requested by the team.

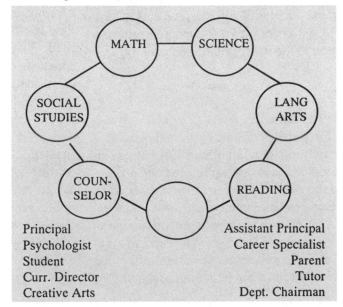

Principal
Psychologist
Student
Curr. Director
Creative Arts

Assistant Principal
Career Specialist
Parent
Tutor
Dept. Chairman

Results

The direct benefits derived from the daily free-wheeling exchanges that characterize the "huddle" follow.

1. **Rapid recognition of individual student needs.**

   Through discussions at team meetings, and with the counselor as a regular participant, a sharing of information has produced quick identification and a variance of solutions to student problems.

   T. Q. (teacher quote) *Getting to know the students better has been the most impressive thing.*

2. **Increased consistency in discipline techniques.**

   The "huddle" enables communication between teachers regarding specific behavior problems and a sharing of techniques for correction.

   T. Q. *Freedom of grouping procedures within teams enables us to adjust classes, and separate cliques and disruptive students.*

3. **More continuity in subject areas.**

   The "huddle" enables coordination of common units such as:

   T. Q. *Spelling words come from all subject areas. Science and English combine forces to do a science fiction unit or simply coordinate assignments for dual credit. (Example: note taking in English used for extra credit in Math or Science)*

4. **Elimination of assignment duplication.**

   Teachers communicate homework assignments and correlate projects to eliminate having the student do the same task, such as writing an autobiography simultaneously in more than one class.

5. **Coordination of teaching procedures and sharing of materials and techniques.**

   Instructors share techniques, improving and expanding the "How do you do it" methodology phase of instruction.

   T. Q. *It's most interesting to learn how others are presenting material.*

   Unselfishness in sharing materials, specific teaching procedures, and disciplinary techniques has been another positive aspect of the team planning period .

   T. Q. *We share.*

6. **Increased understanding of the student as a person.**

   Teachers get to know students more rapidly and students seem to more readily "open up" and share their problems.

   T. Q. *Improved guidance coordination and utilization have benefited both the student and teacher.*

Through the sharing of information and observation of student reaction to the varied teaching styles of individual team members, the teacher can more quickly focus in on specific learning needs of a particular student. Negative student response to particular procedures can be noted, discussed, and avoided .

T. Q. *Getting to know the students better has been the most impressive thing.*

7. Better administrative communication.

Though the "huddle," the principal can participate in and observe the development of units, the ironing out of team problems, and the beginning of new ideas. This involvement with the ongoing process of team activities lends itself to a more accurate understanding of teacher needs and a freer exchange of ideas.

P. Q. (Principal quote) *Attendance and participation at team meetings enables me as principal to be an integral part of the ongoing academic activities in the classroom, as it should be.*

8. Capitalization by teachers on expertise of specialists.

The school psychologist, speech and hearing assistant, career education specialist, and secondary director all have contributed their expertise to aid in solutions of specific problems when needed.

9. Communication with parents.

Early identification of student needs has produced more frequent and timely contact with parents. If they desire, parents are given the opportunity, through the "huddle," to meet with all members of the team simultaneously. Teachers have also made use of the portable conference telephone to conduct team conference calls with hard to reach parents.

10. Flexible scheduling of academic time based on need.

Through team cooperation and coordination, individual class periods can be lengthened, shortened, or eliminated altogether to provide time for extended lab work, guest speakers, or perhaps field experiences.

T. Q. *Flexible scheduling has greatly helped laboratory work.*

11. Counselor utilization.

As an integral part of the team and an active participant in the daily "huddle," counselors find that their advice and assistance in all phases of team planning are accepted and natural. Vastly improved awareness of the guidance function has been the result. Teacher requests for guidance assistance have increased markedly, and overall awareness of what is happening in the classroom on the part of the counselor has spelled greatly improved services to students.

C. Q. (Counselor quote) *Teachers are now much more aware of what to do, and I feel a real part of what they do.*

12. Interdisciplinary Teaching

A. Teachers, along with counselors and specialists, have fused teaching techniques to execute common units with career guidance providing the common thread.

C. Q. (Counselor quote) *For instance, what better place to develop personalities than in a science unit on heredity and environment.*

B. Language arts and history are now intertwined as *The Diary of Ann Frank* and *Light in the Forest* take on new meaning when team taught in conjunction with World War 11 and the French and Indian War.

C. Another example of total team teaching features a student-produced travel brochure. This team conceived unit kicked off with one of our art teachers featured in a class on purpose, design, and color, includes letters to Chambers of Commerce (language arts), identification and visits to points of interest (social studies), construction of a trip budget and itinerary (math), and analysis of Ohio wildlife parks and recreation areas (science).

D. With one of the top-rated career education programs in Ohio, many teams use career information and guidance as a common thread in planning integrated team taught units. Budgeting an imaginary income (math), using newspapers (reading), and filling out job applications, climaxed by mock interviews are some examples of one of Kimpton's 7th grade career units.

T. Q. *Teaching together has increased student interest, added continuity, and increased students' opportunity to succeed.*

Conclusion

In our welcoming letter to students, we state that along with concentration on the old three R's of reading, writing, and arithmetic, we hope to blend responsibility, respect, and consideration. We feel that our team organizational structure allows the opportunity to provide acceptance, guidance, and social situations necessary for our students to move toward realization of their maximum personal potential. The nucleus of this structure is our "huddle," as this is where we feel we can make it all begin to happen. ▲

The Best in the West

Being a West Winger
It is really great.
Our colors are ones
Even I couldn't hate.

The way we found
    our colors
Was from the lockers
    in the hall.
For they are blue
    and green
And we love them,
    one and all.

Mrs. Eoff, Mrs. Baggs,
    Ms. Speer and
    Maning, too
We wouldn't have a team
If it wasn't for all of you.

The way we got our name
Is very obvious.
It's from the
    side of school
With classes just for us.

If you ever doubt us
Give us a test
You'll see for yourself
We're "The Best
    in the West."

— A seventh grade
    student in Illinois

Knowing and Sharing Self

One of the first steps in the process of teaming is for teachers to decide what they should share about themselves. The following list of questions and statements will help you develop the areas you wish to share.

1. What are my personal and professional strengths?

2. What are the professional areas where I need help or support?

3. What are my personal idiosyncrasies the team must know so they may work well with me?

4. What are my personal goals, i.e., my career goals? What do I want our middle school to be?

Develop endings for the following statements and share.

1. I understand best when

2. I learn easiest when

3. I teach best when

4. I feel I'm a successful teacher when

5. It bothers me when

6. The professional growth area I need to concentrate on is

7. What I need most from this team is

There Is No Finish Line

FRANCINE BUCKINGHAM, LUCILLE JORDAN, SHIRLEY SPANGLER

The story of a successful interdisciplinary unit built around the Olympics that was carried out by "amateurs."

When the Dublin, Ohio, Middle School faculty agreed to embrace a middle school philosophy, many middle school concepts needed to be tried and accepted or rejected. The teachers readily agreed they wanted to provide a "wide variety of opportunities for learning—instructional activities designed to allow students maximum opportunity to interact with peers, teachers and outside resources in a real world atmosphere." But how?

Implementing this particular concept soon involved interdisciplinary units. The interdisciplinary team, composed of a math, science, social studies, and language arts teacher, agreed upon a philosophy of instruction and major goals to be addressed. The team agreed to try two units during the first year. One of these units, the most successful one, was titled "There Is No Finish Line." The theme which tied together the many subjects was the Olympics. A description of how this interdisciplinary team created a high degree of excitement for learning on the part of the students follows.

7:30 a.m. in the dark, chilly hours two teachers and a student light a torch while standing in front of a police car..

9:00 in the evening, a teacher sews ribbons on medals by the light of the pop machine while others sort and view slides for a closing ceremony...

9:30 mid-morning, 150 students run in place, chanting to music while teachers huff and puff to keep going. . .

Late morning, a swimming pool fills with 150 screaming eighth grade transescents...

11:30 at night, a teacher roams Dublin shining his flashlight in search of mile-markers. . . All of these scenes took place as the interdisciplinary unit evolved.

Rationale and Results

When designing this interdisciplinary unit the fundamental concern was the developmental needs of transescents. Because of rapid physical development, a vital curricular area for transescents is health education, hence the decision to explore the XXIII Olympic Games as well as lifetime physical fitness. This unit integrated all subject areas. The use of a web to map out connectors aided in planning. The approach used enabled teachers to connect goals and link student needs to interests and prior learning experiences. Instead of nine 40 minute periods, the team utilized various blocks of time to accomplish the varied activities planned.

A pre-test was given to determine how much students knew about mental and physical

93

fitness and to assess their attitudes. A post-test measured the change in student attitudes and understandings. Results of the pre- and post-tests showed that a third of the students increased their understanding of personal physical fitness and their awareness of how lifetime physical fitness can improve life. A change of attitudes was clear.

Teachers and students were both very enthusiastic about the active instruction provided. The effort to accommodate different learning styles resulted in activities which motivated students and eliminated discipline problems.

The use of a web to map out connectors between subjects aided planning.

Implementation
The unit activities planned accomplished many listed objectives from the Dublin Middle School graded courses of study, such as the development of visual literacy skills, the use of the writing process, and learning to think creatively and critically. Many other objectives emerged as the unit developed and various activities were suggested.

In health and science classes, students watched tapes of the Olympics and viewed themselves performing, comparing norms for their ages and weight with those of professionals. Agility, blood-pressure, stress, physical reaction, heart rate, and physical endurance tests were studied. The Special Olympics were also studied.

The effort to meet learning styles resulted in activities that motivated students and improved discipline.

The kinesthetic learning style was utilized when the students constructed a 3-D mural, which integrated all subject areas. In history classes, students drew a time line, which provided the background for a fifteen foot mural. In health and science classes students made three dimensional objects depicting the athletes and sports of various time periods. In language arts classes students placed the objects on the mural in the appropriate time period. The finished product was hung in the commons and viewed by the entire student body.

After the language arts classes completed the mural, they researched and wrote about famous sports personalities. The students also entered the contest *Quest For Gold,* sponsored by the Stuart Hall Company, and each wrote a 150 word composition, "How Competition Can Make You a Better Person." Here they were able to express their personal thoughts and make use of the writing process. They read and performed a play about Billy Mills called "Running Brave" in classes and also created a universal dictionary. The aim of the latter was to produce a dictionary that could be utilized by all nationalities. Brainstorming helped to determine the necessary vocabulary and social language that would be needed to travel in a foreign country. Students produced an intriguing picture/symbol product.

In math classes the manipulative activities, boomerang-can and a paper-length cutting contest, gave students opportunities to experience mathematics. Calculating sports scores and solving Olympic-related story problems reinforced the mathematical concepts of computation and problem-solving. Creating a protective box for an egg, which could be dropped from the roof of a building without breaking the egg, provided critical problem solving.

History students researched the ancient Olympics, discussed and debated the political issues of terrorism, Hitler's aggression, and Russian-U.S.A. relations. They also made predictions about future Olympic games. They shared in the making of the timeline and reproduced flags of the Olympic countries participating in the Los Angeles games. At the same time, Spanish classes studied the history of the Olympics in Spain, Spanish sports, notable athletes of the Hispanic world, and identified Spanish words by playing the game of vocabulary baseball.

An Olympic closing ceremony provided closure for the unit.

Designated days promoted team identification throughout the study of the unit. The special days included Button Day, when students designed and made their own buttons. Team Shirt Day was the result of a contest to choose the team name, *Fleet Feet,* and the logo, a tennis shoe. Team members could be recognized by other students in the school by their apparel on Sweat Suit Day.

To provide closure for the unit, the team simulated an Olympic closing ceremony. Videotapes and slides of the many events and experiences were shown, and school administrators presented sixty gold, silver, and bronze medals to students.

Community Partnerships

Police, city government, and parents cooperated with the school to make the "kick off" of the unit a success. The opening ceremonies included a marathon through town with students and teachers participating, a balloon release, the lighting of the Olympic torch, and making *Fleet Feet* identity buttons.

City officials and parents were involved in a big "kick-off."

Visits to the Sawmill Athletic Club and The Ohio State University promoted education/business partnership for two days. At the athletic club, students observed and were given instruction in how physical fitness can fit into one's life after school is completed. They also participated in volleyball, racquetball, swimming, and aerobics. They were taught to ice skate at OSU and watched a Dublin Middle School student, an Olympic hopeful, perform.

Another field experience was a trip to the Center of Science and Industry in Columbus, Ohio, where students watched a special sports science presentation. Students reacted with, "Gee, I didn't know size wasn't important to overpower a person," and "You can actually throw an egg from that distance and it didn't break!"

Conclusion

Daily journals reflected the student evaluation of the program: ... "Why can't school always be as much fun as this"; ... "I learned a lot of stuff in this unit"; ... "I hated to see it all end and go back to the regular classes and schedule"; ... "What's the next unit going to be?"...

This interdisciplinary unit implemented the tenets of teaming. Coordinated planning and organization of the instructional program took place as teachers created new ways to deliver curriculum. Teachers agreed on desirable academic and behavioral expectations for their students, and evidences of undesirable behavior were dramatically decreased. A sense of community was developed by students and teachers. This positive experience resulted in a second interdisciplinary unit on flight and encouraged teachers to develop mini units that involved only two or three disciplines. ▲

"Why can't school always be as much fun as this."

"What's the next unit going to be?"

Flexible Scheduling Can Be Hectic!

On Friday, January 13, the Discoverer Team had Teacher Swap Day on the flip-flop schedule with a switch of the English and Geography classrooms, coinciding with the Martin Luther King Assemblies, held during the real 2nd and 6th hours of our team time (actually our 5th and 3rd hour times). During our 6th hour, which is really 3rd, Mr. Blackman, our Health Teacher, who on that day was our Reading Resource Teacher, came around to tell our kids that on Tuesday, after the King Holiday, we would run the reversed flip-flop schedule, but not to bring books to the real 2nd hour, since we would be going to the cafeteria for a team assembly then split the remaining time between 2nd and 3rd hours and have no Tiger Pride session. Our substitute, Mrs. Andrews, who was subbing for Miss Sherwin, our English teacher who swapped with our l.D. Resource Person for the day, held up quite well. By the way, so did the kids!

Carol McGehe
Urbana Middle School.

The Interdisciplinary Unit — It's Here to Stay!

JOANNE KEREKES

I.D.U's brought the past to life and life to teachers in this New Jersey school where resource units became a way of life.

I don't remember the Cuban Missile Crisis, the Korean War, the year Hawaii became a state, or even "American Bandstand." I whiled away my hours playing with dolls and watching "Howdy Doody."

As an educator, however, I have been fortunate to be able to experience some of the more memorable events of the 50s. I have dressed up in my mother's dresses and jitterbugged and strolled my way across the school cafeteria. I have "droodled," hula-hooped, and been one of sixteen other teachers crammed into a phone booth.

Where were you when John F. Kennedy was killed? When was the last time that you dressed like a hippie? When did you last participate in a love-in? Surely you have not forgotten the promise of Kennedy's Camelot? The pride of winning the space race? The emotions of the Civil Rights Movement? The love beads, gum wrapper chains, and lapel buttons? If you haven't thought about any of these things since the sixties, you are missing something. Not everyone can pick a part of the past and relive its most characteristic and memorable moments; but those of us involved in middle school education can!

In the past five years, I have been a 20s flapper, a "have-not" in the midst of a world hunger crisis, a host of "What's My Line?. . . Monster Style," and a calligrapher at a Renaissance Fair. And these are just some of the places in time to which I, along with the staff and students of the Grace N. Rogers Middle School in Hightstown, New Jersey, have journeyed, thanks to the interdisciplinary unit.

To travel to such hard to reach places we have used as our "vehicle" the Interdisciplinary Unit (I.D.U.), a short-term, intensive unit of study based on a particular theme. Such units are often called thematic units.

The I.D.U. has gradually become a part of the fabric of our middle school. Experimentation here with the concept began over six years ago and we now have an extensive and varied menu of such units occurring throughout the year. This article will seek to explain why the I.D.U. had ignited such interest and why it has fueled enough energy to inspire staff to develop new units of study each year.

I.D.U.'s. . . What are they?

We distinguish Interdisciplinary Units from interdisciplinary teaching. We use the term interdisciplinary teaching to refer to that which occurs when the regular curriculum being taught provides for a natural overlap between subject areas and when students can see the relevance and the inter-relatedness of their disciplines. Students are thereby assisted in seeing the content areas as pieces of a whole rather than as separate entities.

This correlative approach to teaching is best illustrated by the use of themes in social studies which can then serve as springboards for the literature and writing that students cover in the reading and language arts classes. For example, as students study minorities in social studies under the theme, "A Search for Conscience," they might be studying such novels as *Acorn People, The Diary of Anne Frank,* or *A Raisin in the Sun* and writing plays, autobiographies, and diaries based on these readings. Interdisciplinary teaching, as we view it, is a long-term, ongoing approach to curriculum that requires teachers to share their plans and topics and be ready to correlate wherever possible.

The I.D.U. also stresses the interrelationships between subject areas. However, the focus of it is a separately selected theme, not necessarily related to any one subject area's regular curriculum.

Interdisciplinary units:

- provide students with an in-depth, short term focus on a particular topic;

- generate strong student/staff interest and motivation; and

- involve students, staff, and parents in the curriculum development and decision-making processes.

They elicit considerable enthusiasm among staff and students over a short period of time. They are meant to be fun and a break from the traditional pattern of study. But the amount of knowledge acquired or the understanding ingrained is substantial and significant.

Scheduling and Developing the I.D.U.
An I.D.U. is best when it is implemented at a time when students' interest in school is traditionally at a low point, the days preceding a holiday, the final days of the school year, the days prior to a vacation, or the days following a major testing period. By changing the pace and raising the interest level, students become involved almost without realizing it, and learn a great deal. When appropriately scheduled, an I.D.U. is a very productive and meaningful use of time.

After six years we have an extensive menu of resource units.

An I.D.U. is best implemented at a time when students' interest in school is traditionally at a low point.

A key to success when first experimenting with I.D.U.'s is to find a topic that is of mutual interest to both students and the teachers involved. Thus you will have a built-in motivating factor and a positive climate from the start. One of the first units of study we developed was entitled the "Fabulous Fifties." The students were quickly "into" the 50s clothing and rock and roll; the teachers liked the nostalgia.

After selecting a few basic objectives for the unit, we began brainstorming a wide variety of both large and small group activities. These activities had to have educational merit as well as entertainment value. Since parent/student/teacher interaction was one of the objectives, many activities included parent participation. We then narrowed down our list of events, developed a schedule, and regrouped students into non-traditional groupings in order to break their normal routine. Each of the teachers in the team assumed responsibility for developing and/or organizing some of the planned events. Two members also served as coordinators. Considerable research and planning would be required of all.

The kick-off was an assembly during which the entire team was informed about the unit and its objectives. It was extremely important that students understand the several educational goals of the I.D.U. We also explained the tentative schedule and distributed trivia quizzes which were to be completed by the students and their parents.

The "business" portion of the assembly was followed by a faculty band playing selections from the 50s as teachers modeled various 50s fashions. Next came a slide show depicting a "walk through the decade." The slides highlighted key facts about each year—from the historical and social to each year's top dance, the most popular television show, hit song, and best selling novel. Interspersed among actual 50s pictures were slides of the team's staff reenacting in humorous fashion various 50s fads, sporting events, and foibles. (The students said that the slides were really copacetic!) The assembly concluded with a 50s sing-a-long with the faculty up on stage singing and dancing and with the students following along with their 50s songbooks.

By the end of the assembly, the needed tone had been set. The students and staff were ready to enjoy a special learning experience. At this point the staff realized how important a "kick-off" activity was to the I.D.U.; it informed, motivated, and provided a send-off for the sessions that followed.

Students then entered into three days of classes during which time they studied each of their regular disciplines but with a 50s twist.

The kick-off for the Fabulous Fifties unit was an assembly during which the entire team was informed about the unit and its objectives — and then came music, dance, and costumes!

Examples were 50s lingo in language arts, Fins of the Fifties in science, air raid drills and bomb shelters in social studies, a 50s shopping spree in math, and a production of "Twelve Angry Men" in reading.

The unit culminated with a day of 50s fads and fashions. Students selected from such activities as Droodles, Hula-Hoops, Cramming, Egg Cream Making, and Crossword Competition. Students also spent this day dressed in 50s fashions in preparation for the sock hop which was held that evening. Students, staff, and parents all danced and tried their hands at the Broom Dance, the Multiplication Dance, and the Limbo.

In the weeks that followed the I.D.U., the students and staff reminisced about the excitement and the fun. The staff was glad that the unit had been completed just prior to winter vacation; a week was needed to recuperate! But, despite the exhaustion, we knew we had discovered something powerful and exciting about middle school education. We had also learned from our mistakes and we used this knowledge when preparing future units.

I.D.U.'s . . . The Aftermath

Following the fifties unit, we continued to develop and experiment with I.D.U.'s throughout the remainder of the school year. Our school board, the East Windsor Board of Education, was introduced to the concept of I.D.U.'s at a board presentation during which time the members were walked through a unit. They responded with much enthusiasm and provided us with a grant to further develop additional I.D.U.'s during the summer and to begin to train staff in our sister middle school. That summer and in the years that followed, staff development began and units were written on various cognitive levels.

Some units were geared primarily toward academics such as the "Newspaper," ". . . And Justice for All" (Law and Order), and "Propaganda." Some were developed in order for students to experience bygone periods of time such as the "Roaring 20s," the "60s," and the "Elizabethan Era." Still others were written with more abstract goals in mind such as "World Hunger," "The Changing Family" (which later became the springboard of our family life curriculum), and "Heroes."

All of our units have been carefully developed and revised and enriched with each successive use. Every resource unit includes a rationale, list of objectives, suggested time frame (usually 2-5 days) and schedule, several introductory activities, an accumulation of interdisciplinary activities, and an assortment of culminating events. We also include pre-reading for teachers, a bibliography, and a materials/A.V. list. This type of documentation enables anyone to pick up a unit and implement it. Phone calls between the two middle schools in our district are common occurrences now as we share our ideas and resources. I.D.U.'s have provided us with a common bond.

Guidelines for Success

Certainly we ran into a number of roadblocks along the way in I.D.U. development and learned by experience. The following pointers should be kept in mind when working on an I.D.U.:

• Educate parents and students as to what an I.D.U. is and as to what its objectives are. For parents this can be accomplished via a newsletter or at a parent meeting. For students, the introductory assembly helps to set the stage.

• Train staff in I.D.U. development gradually. Start with brainstorming techniques, interest surveys, and perhaps only one unit a year.

• Select a topic of mutual interest to staff and students to insure success and pave the way for more complex units.

• Keep costs to a minimum. (Most of our units cost less than $50.00 to implement.)

• Grade level teams, common team planning time, and block scheduling are essential for I.D.U. development.

• Select one or two coordinators to oversee the entire unit and insure its cohesiveness.

• Publicize your I.D.U.'s. They are unique. Help the community to recognize and appreciate the place they have in middle school education.

• Document everything you do; committing your thoughts to writing is one sure way to preserve the "meat" of an I.D.U.

Educate parents and students as to what an I.D.U. is and what its objectives are.

The Future of I.D.U.'s

We continued to develop units as the need and interest arose. Such as "The New York Experience," "African Cultures," and a "Health Fair." Grade level teams do two to three I.D.U.'s a year and participate in one to two units as a school. Increased common team planning time is further enabling us to develop even more units and to widen our knowledge of their innerworkings.

In East Windsor, I.D.U.'s are here to stay. The students enjoy them, the parents understand their objectives, the teachers develop them (and therefore feel a strong commitment toward them), and the school board and administration enthusiastically support them. Quite simply, we all believe in them.

Why not get your grade level team or middle school staff together and try an I.D.U. It will lift your spirits and might transport you and your students back to the days of Al Capone, the first talkies, flag pole sitting and Shipwreck Kelly, prohibition, or the first Miss America Pageant. ▲

Interdisciplinary planning is enhanced by having a "work place" for the team.

The Simulation Technique Applied in an Ancient Egypt I.D.U.

ROBERT B. STROMBERG, JOAN M. SMITH

A format for an I.D.U. that involves students extensively is described in this chronicle of a successful implementation.

The learning process at the middle school level may be greatly enhanced through the simulation technique. According to Kindred (1978), ". . . simulations can be defined as a teaching technique that uses or creates 'real life' situations through games, role playing, or sociodramas, generally with decision-making involvement of the participants during and at end of the program." Such a technique gains the attention and interest of students, and gives them a chance to physically as well as mentally create an environment which is being studied (Stromberg, 1980).

This article describes the steps in the simulation technique which provides a format that teachers can apply to their own units. The role of the teacher and the students are outlined and explained.

In the second part, these steps in the simulation technique are applied to a simulation on Ancient Egypt developed at the Galvin Middle School in Canton, Massachusetts.

This model can be considered a student-centered and interactive model in which the teacher acts as a facilitator. The only exception would be the teacher's role at the beginning of the simulation to provide the needed structure, and possibly later in the simulation in the formulation of testing and evaluation.

Teacher Roles

Teacher involvement in the simulation model consists of explaining, refereeing, coaching, and discussing. In the process of *explaining,* the teacher should clarify the process of the simulation without providing too much information. As in the case of real life situations, not all the information is provided at the beginning of the situation. However, the initial information must be sufficient to make the simulation operational. It is implied that the student will become "more aware" as the simulation progresses.

The teacher's role of *refereeing* is to assure that the students are following the intended simulation process. This is not to imply that the teacher directs each step of the process, but rather serves as an "overseer" of the progression of the simulation. For example, if grouping is necessary, it is important that the teacher make sure that the groups are heterogeneously structured.

The third role of the teacher is *coaching*. In this capacity, the teacher can provide advice, direction and the important positive support. The teacher should not actively participate, but rather provide support and necessary information, which may be actively or passively requested by the students. The teacher must be sensitive to the climate of the simulation and provide stimulation if the process is dragging.

The final role of the teacher comes at the end of the simulation. This involves the teacher as a leader of a *discussion* of the simulation. The classroom discussion should center around the perceptions of the students concerning the "real world" implications of the simulation. This may include drawing parallels with real life situations as well as suggestions for improving the simulation.

The teacher serves more as a coach than an instructor. The major roles belong to the students.

Although the teacher is important, the major roles in the simulation belong to the students. They will experience many of the following roles: organizer, planner, experimenter, creator, decision maker, and follower.

As the groups are formed and work is assigned, the students must first consider the organization of material. The demand of the material might force the students to select a leader or leaders of the group so that organization can be better facilitated. Once the organization is accomplished, the need for planning is evident. In most simulations, time constraints will force groups to plan wisely.

In the process of planning, the members of the group have to engage in decision making. In a heterogeneous group, it might be assumed that the higher ability students would affect the decision making process the most. However, in many cases, popularity of certain group members and some average common sense usually win.

In planning students have to engage in decision-making.

As the simulation progresses and the students feel a little more at ease, the processes of creating and experimenting usually develop. Examples of the culture being studied are displayed with pride. In some cases, there is a healthy competition among groups to produce the best examples of drawings, maps, charts, and artifacts of the culture.

In the group process of the simulation, the students also learn to be good followers. When conflict occurs in the decision and planning process, the teacher (in the role of referee) should encourage students to be understanding and respectful of the ideas of others.

This behavior can be reinforced by indicating that those who lead are the most effective leaders and they have also been the best followers. This is an extremely important nurturing effect of the group process.

It is unrealistic to assume that the students will have exclusively positive experiences throughout the group process of the simulation. A healthy atmosphere of interaction and conflict will produce a more realistic feeling of the real world and be more educative.

In the final segment of the simulation the students develop a better feel for the culture studied, as well as a better understanding of themselves. Understanding the lives of others, and the problems which they had to contend with on a daily basis should increase the students' ability to feel as if they were members of the culture studied.

The Theory Applied

A re-creation of Ancient Egypt came to life in the sixth grade area of the Galvin Middle School in Canton, Massachusetts. Far from the simplicity of "normal" school projects, the sixth grade students and teachers created a life sized simulation of a pyramid measuring 27' x 22' x 8'. The pyramid housed five tomb chambers complete with illustrations depicting the lives of four pharaohs and one queen.

The entrance way of the "Great Pyramid," which conspicuously protruded into the hallway from the double classroom, was the center of attention to students and faculty. Upon entering, all were amazed at the dramatic transformation of the classrooms into a life sized replica of the inside of the "Great Pyramid." Encircling the tomb chambers, a "secret" passageway was constructed to heighten the intrigue.

The sixth grade classes were divided into groupings of five or six students. Each group was charged with the task of writing a term paper on Ancient Egypt with an understanding of the interrelationships among the five major disciplines. The major discipline teachers aided the students) in the understanding of Ancient Egypt in their subject areas.

In social studies class, the students were introduced to the three kingdoms, the lives of the pharaohs and queens, the myths of the gods and goddesses, the writing of hieroglyphs, and the life style of the Egyptians.

Math students were introduced to Egyptian numeration. They studied the history of the symbols and utilization of these symbols in the everyday life of the Egyptians.

> A re-creation of Ancient Egypt came to life in the sixth grade area.

> The students were divided into groups of five or six to complete an interdisciplinary assignment.

In English class, students read and discussed the book *Wrapped in Eternity* and learned related vocabulary words. Material from this book reinforced many of the concepts explored in social studies.

Science students created models of the Nile Valley area and studied topography, latitude, longitude, map scale, map size and erosion. Further topics included levers, fulcrums, and early machines as well as diseases of ancient Egypt, ecology, and nutrition of the area. Canopic jars were fashioned from papier maché by the students and added to the tomb rooms of the pyramid.

Reading students studied words and terms growing out of the unit as well as the organization and mechanics of a term paper.

Six weeks were needed to complete the unit.

The duration of the entire unit was six weeks. The construction of the Great Pyramid with tomb chamber and Nile River Valley area was accomplished in the first two weeks. Students and teachers worked on the "framing" of the pyramid during and after school. On the frames of 2" x 4"s, large pieces of construction paper were placed and students decorated the "walls" throughout the simulation unit. Classes were assigned to work on a specific tomb chamber representing the life of a particular pharaoh.

A group of students from each class translated the pharaoh's life history into hieroglyphs (this is no easy task even for experienced egyptologists). The walls of each tomb chamber were covered with three inch high hieroglyphs representing the translation. As was the case in the actual Egyptian tombs, a rainbow of colors was used to beautify the hieroglyphic symbols (to help out the many visitors, the English translation was also displayed). On the remaining walls of each of the tomb chambers, drawings of important events and artifacts enhanced the pharaoh's life history. Each of the classes worked on the construction in a cooperative effort and shared in their excitement as each tomb chamber took form. Each day students were allowed to "spend time" in the secret passageway to increase their feelings of excitement in the mystery of the pyramid.

Students translated pharaohs' lives into hieroglyphs.

A special day was set aside as "Egyptian Day" when the term papers were completed. Much preparation and attention were given to design of Egyptian costumes. Students as well as teachers proudly wore their costumes for the entire day. During the day, the students acted as tour guides for eager students from other classes. Descriptions were given by the tour guides as to methods of pyramid construction, arrangement of tomb chambers and history of the pharaohs. Tour guides were also stationed in the Nile River Valley area next to the "Great Pyramid" to describe the scientific developments of the Egyptians.

Arrangements were made in the school cafeteria for an "Egyptian Festival" luncheon, complete with ancient food and entertainment. Examples of ancient Egyptian artifacts were shown and discussed in a slide presentation presented by a representative from the Boston Museum of Fine Arts.

A special parents' night was organized. Students and teachers again wore their Egyptian costumes and tours of the "Great Pyramid" were proudly given. Parents had a chance to view their children's hard work in the tombs and in the term papers.

Culminating activities involved many special events with other students and parents.

The tomb chamber which drew the most attention was King Tut's. As in the case of the other tomb chambers, King Tut's tomb chamber had the life history of the pharaoh translated into hieroglyphs and pictures covering the walls. The special attraction was a six foot sarcophagus and mummy in the middle of the chamber. The sarcophagus itself was made of 2" plywood and 2" x 3"s and decorated with symbols and pictures of those "things" most revered by King Tut. The mummy was made from a clothing store mannequin wrapped with strips of old bed sheets.

Students carefully explained to visitors that the internal organs of King Tut were not in their "usual place," but proudly displayed in canopic jars which were built into the walls of the tomb chamber.

This tomb chamber, in particular reflected the mysterious spirit of the ancient Egyptian tombs. There were times when students actually "felt" the presence of King Tut!

The success of this simulation was evident. Positive responses were overwhelming. The enthusiasm and interest of the students proved its educational value. Many students who were classified as ''slow learners'' produced as well as other students and, in some cases, even better. The physical building of the simulation and the experiencing of the *environment* of the area studied generated interest for all students. Not to be overlooked, of course, is the substantial body of new knowledge acquired along with an increased perspective on life.

The relatively new development of the simulation technique at the middle school level may prove to be a viable force in future planning of middle school curricula. Its success at the Galvin Middle School certainly gives strength to its future consideration. ▲

References

Kindred, Leslie et al. *The Middle School Curriculum: A Practitioner's Handbook.* Boston: Allyn & Bacon 1978.

Stromberg, Robert B. "Social Studies Simulation in the Middle School Classroom" *Dissemination Services on the Middle Grades XI:6* 1980.

Types of Instructional Collaboration As Observed in Functioning Teams

Random Reinforcement

A teacher is aware of a concept, skill, topic, etc. that the students have studied in another class and makes reference to it or uses it as an example in the course of teaching a lesson within his/her own class.

Skill Reinforcement

A teacher is aware of a skill that another teacher has taught and incorporates ways for students to use it in his/her class. The teacher does not teach the skill but does provide opportunities for students to apply it in a different subject context.

Skill Instruction Collaboration

Two or more teachers determine an area of skill emphasis needed by their students and then jointly plan and implement instructional activities within their classes to address the skill.

Subject Content Integration

Two or more teachers identify units or topics within their subject content that are related and then jointly plan and implement lessons which take advantage of the relationship (e.g., the story of Johnny Tremaine is studied in English while the history class is studying the revolutionary war.)

Interdisciplinary Unit

The team teachers develop and implement a unit of study based upon a central theme. Whole team and individual class activities are conducted to support the unit.

Developed by John Meinke and Gene Pickler, Orange County Public Schools, Orlando, FL.

Interdisciplinary Units: Keystones of Learning

Timothy Daniels, Joseph O'Brien, Robert Pittman

Three examples of interdisciplinary units that give Richardson Middle School its special flavor are described in this article.

Raucous treble laughter mixed with a few future baritone guffaws echoes in the river basin. Joseph O'Brien, seventh grade English teacher, struggles to regain his footing among the rocks on the creek bottom as his hip boots ship water. "Dive, dive," yells a chorus of voices from the bank.

A group of twelve seventh graders, following their teachers with characteristic loyalty, end up hopelessly lost in downtown Philadelphia. The group's destination was to be restored Colonial Philadelphia. The group's location, for most of one day, is a Victorian-style candy store. Vince Cianfaro and his charges have missed a turn and end up in the wrong historical period. Candy sales are high.

Double disaster strikes a group of teacher and student explorers at Pocono Environmental Educational Center. Hank Bohinick leads a game group up a small mountain only to discover that the wrong hill has been climbed, while another teacher lies in the sick bay for two days. The students on the trip not only survive but proclaim the entire environmental education trip a success. Strangely, teachers agree.

All of the foregoing teacher predicaments and accompanying student joy might sound a bit unusual, but to those used to working with early adolescents they are perhaps too familiar. Because these scenes and sounds are the products and by-products of teachers and students interacting on new ideas and projects, successes and mistakes abound. Risk-taking is a must.

All of these teacher/student situations have occurred in the context of interdisciplinary units (IDU's) at Richardson Middle School. IDU's are the mainstay of teaming at Richardson, a 5-8 school of 1,000 students.

Teaming at Richardson Middle School

Teaming here is simply a group of teachers working together to coordinate the instructional program. A math, science, English, and social studies teacher make up each "team." There are two teams of approximately one hundred students each in the sixth, seventh, and eighth grade. Within each team students receive instruction in the four academic areas. In sixth grade, students remain with their team for a fifth period of reading taught by all of the team teachers.

Teaming is not synonymous with team teaching. Traditionally, team teaching involves two or more faculty teaching together at the same time. At Richardson, teaming connotes coordinated planning and organization of the instructional program not necessarily the actual sharing of a particular instructional responsibility.

Joint planning and organization of the instructional program includes many things besides the consideration of subject matter. For example, a guidance counselor attends one of each team's twice-weekly meetings to help with student concerns and problems. Also, each team leader spends much time on organizing for team pictures, team T-shirts, team elections, etc. But the single most important and time consuming team task is the construction and implementation of required interdisciplinary units (IDU's).

Teams spend 30-40% of their two weekly planning periods on organizing IDU's.

Logs of team meetings indicate that teams spend between 30% to 40% of their two meetings per week planning and organizing IDU's. Four approved IDU's are required of each team every year. However, most teams plan and conduct between five and seven projects.

IDU's are also the most professionally motivating aspect of teaming at Richardson. They give team members a sense of purpose and a reason for being a team. Cooperating is the byline of teachers, who frequently take 100 students on field trips, set up large displays, and conduct large scale activities under the interested eyes of the public. The need for interaction causes interaction; ergo cooperation.

The three IDU's described as follows are teacher constructed. Each reflects the current curriculum at our middle school. One of the main criteria for administrative approval of each IDU is the match of the IDU with school district curriculum in two or more academic subjects.

IDU's give team members a sense of purpose and a reason for being a team.

Each IDU is described in three categories:

1) **Rationale:**   Why should the IDU be conducted?
                     How does it reflect the curriculum?

2) **Objectives:**   What will students accomplish by participating
                     in the IDU?

3) **Nuts 'n Bolts:** How is the IDU organized?
                       How are problems avoided
                       (Murphy's Laws)?

I. WATER: AN ECOLOGICAL STUDY

Rationale - This IDU originally developed through a shared concern for water conservation, and the realization that the vast majority of our students took their water supply for granted. By tracing Crum Creek (the source of our local water) through Delaware County, PA., and by visiting the Springfield Water Company, the instructors hoped to make the students more aware of the precious natural resource of water.

Objectives - This IDU is interdisciplinary and reflects all four academic areas; however, the main objective comes from the science and social studies areas. Both disciplines include ecology in the seventh grade. In addition, the science curriculum calls for all students to use the scientific method through labs and experiments called "investigations." This water IDU combines the scientific approach with the pollution and ecology units already covered.

The math teacher had the students make quantitative studies of daily water consumption rates, and showed students how to calculate the water bill for their parents, while the English instructor pitched in by having each student pen a letter to the editor on the topic of water conservation—and by floundering about in Crum Creek.

During this IDU, the students had to complete field investigations, mock water bills, water consumption charts, letters to the editor, and water data booklets (which were used for further study back in the classroom).

The water field study was planned with six stops at various sites along the Crum Creek watershed. The IDU required a lot of student involvement—and this, in turn, required a lot of advance preparation.

The students were grouped in work teams of six or seven students. Each work team was responsible for one of the various tests to be performed. Arrangements were made for a guided tour of the Springfield Water Company. The one hundred plus students were divided into two groups. To avoid a crowd scene in the creek, two buses were used, and two separate itineraries were planned.

Teachers planned the investigations to be done at each site. Students were to test for water clarity, water PH, and pollution. They were also to note the presence of life in the stream, and measure the water temperature, air temperature, and the rate of flow of the stream. A sample of water was collected at each site to be brought back to the classroom for further investigation after the field trip.

Both class work and work at field sites characterized this IDU.

111

Practice sessions were held in the classroom and on school grounds. Interview booklets and water consumption worksheets were developed for the students. One teacher was selected to go into the stream with different pairs of students at each site.

Finally, all the teachers agreed to spend one or two days after the trip to wrap-up the project in the classroom. This "wrap-up" involved grading the worksheets, summary reports, water data, letters, and individual test results.

II. MAN AND HIS ENVIRONMENT: A SOCIALIZATION EXPERIMENT

Rationale - The Man and His Environment unit developed from our desire to provide Springfield students with an opportunity to experience the total ecological environment. The vehicle for this experience was to be a three day/two night field trip to the Pocono Environmental Education Center located in the Pocono mountain range of eastern Pennsylvania.

Objectives - Once again the social studies and science curricula provided the basic concepts for this IDU. However, the ecology roots of the unit soon branched out into the other academic areas. The English instructor discovered the positive applications of journal keeping and poetry study during the three day mountain trip, while the math teacher had the students keeping the financial records for themselves and for the team during the eight week fruit sale fund raiser that eventually became an integral part of this project.

The social studies instructor was able to cover map reading skills, orienteering, archaeology, ecology studies and survival skills, while the science teacher incorporated his curriculum into the unit by developing water study experiments, fossil, weather, and wildlife studies, forest ecology lessons, observational hikes, and nature walks.

The Pocono Environmental Education Center offers a comprehensive curriculum that is in itself interdisciplinary. There are twenty-four mini-courses offered at the Center, and our itinerary included nature hikes, wildlife ecology sessions, forest ecology sessions, outdoor science lessons, survival training sessions, nature arts and crafts, fossil trails, braille trails, confidence courses, weather courses, orienteering sessions, astronomy courses, firebuilding instructions, canoe instructions, and the Action Socialization Experiences Course.

These sessions ranged in length from thirty minutes to two hours. The typical day ran from 7:00 A.M. to 10:00 P.M. and included meal breaks, two recreation sessions, and five or six environmental activities.

This IDU was carried out in a three day/two night field trip to the mountains.

Program development led to the problem of staffing. Fortunately, we were able to get twelve parents to come along on the field trip. This community involvement solved our staffing problem.

This IDU faced a financial problem. To help students defray the $45.00 each cost, the team held a citrus fruit sale. Participation was voluntary, but most students were willing and thereby reduced the personal cost of the trip.

III. THE CITY RENAISSANCE

Rationale—This IDU developed from our study of the importance of cities. The close proximity of Philadelphia to the suburban classrooms of Springfield allows students an excellent opportunity to experience the results of an urban renewal project firsthand. This is all the more valuable since the renaissance of Philadelphia's Society Hill and Old City has become a model for the world.

Objectives — The growth of cities is a major theme of study in the seventh grade social studies curriculum. The science curriculum addresses the problems of city inhabitants. Waste management, air pollution, and water pollution are studied as serious threats to society. In English class, letters are sent to major cities throughout the country. These letters pose questions to city planners about the problems they face, and the various ways they try to solve their problems. As the answers trickle back and are filed for future use, the math class works to compute the cost of such major city headaches as transportation, police protection, and sanitation. All four subject areas make ample use of the Philadelphia newspapers—an ideal interdisciplinary textbook.

After a close examination of the problems of modern cities, the task of analyzing solutions to such problems is undertaken. At this point, the various programs of urban renewal are studied — and Philadelphia comes under close scrutiny.

The major vehicle for our in-depth study of Philadelphia is a two-day walking tour of Society Hill and Old City, renewed areas of Philadelphia. Two buses are used, parent volunteers are enlisted, and ten separate walking tours are planned. The students are broken into groups of ten—and each group is off on its own. The in-depth nature of the walking tour gives the students a firsthand experience with the success that Philadelphia has achieved in revitalizing itself. For two days children see an area of the city that is attracting visitors and new residents and proving that a city still can be a good place to live.

Twelve parents joined the group to assist.

An intensive study of Philadelphia was truly interdisciplinary — and contemporary.

113

Conclusion

Interdisciplinary units are given a high priority in teaming at Richardson Middle School. They serve as focal points within each team in the school. Teachers, students, parents and administrators, of necessity, come together to organize and implement each IDU.

Seventh and eighth grade teachers have been teaming for four years. Last year the sixth grade staff demanded to be teamed, too — a good indication of success.

Each year several teams submit proposals for summer workshops on interdisciplinary units, another indication of their validity.

Finally, because of their match with curriculum, and with the nature of early adolescents, IDU's are justifiable in and of themselves. The serendipity of IDU's is the teamwork that they engender. ▲

The serendipity of IDU's is the teamwork that they engender.

Good administrators meet with each team on a regular basis.

The Roaring Twenties— an Interdisciplinary Unit

MELVIN A. BRODSKY

320 eighth graders and 21 teachers re-create and relive the 1920s during five half-days of exciting activities.

The air is thick with nervous excitement and anticipation as the sound of KDKA crackles over the radio (P.A. System). "Welcome to the 1920s" thunders in the ears of 320 eighth graders. One entire floor of the building has been sealed off and magically transformed back in time to the original age of the building, circa 1929. The students realize that very shortly it will be "twenty-three skidoo" and they have to decide which activity to participate in.

As KDKA signs off, organized chaos sets in. Films start to flicker in both of the Bijous; singing and dancing can be heard coming from the Cabaret; the Bear and Bull Markets are overflowing with potential buyers and sellers; *The Daily Blab* is busily trying to run off a special edition; Mae West is deep in conversation with Charlie Chaplin, and John Dillinger and Clyde Barrow are huddled together outside of the bank.

Just as the teachers are approaching the panic stage fearful that the kids are trying to do too much too soon, the whirl of activity starts to finally take on meaning and educational value. Before you can say "Lucky Lindy," the morning is over and students are back in the homerooms listening to a wrap-up of the day's activities over KDKA. Day one has been a real "cat's meow!"

Origin Of The Unit

The Stock Market Game is fairly familiar to schools throughout the country. One of the social studies teachers first included it in the curriculum a dozen years ago. When our conversion to middle school occurred in 1981, the game became the starting point of an interdisciplinary unit involving the social studies and math teachers in eighth grade. Then, during the second year, the language arts teacher wanted to include the literature of the era in the unit, and the science teachers came up with the idea of a Science Fair to further enhance it. By the third year the music, industrial arts, reading, family living, art, and physical education teachers all volunteered suggestions to make the unit even more diversified and comprehensive.

This past year *The Roaring Twenties* included 320 eighth grade students, all three of our eighth grade basic teams, and just about every related arts area in the school. All told, thirty one faculty members were actively involved in the I.D.U. A behemoth had been born!

Organizing The Unit

The Roaring Twenties runs for three and a half consecutive hours for five days. The amount of planning and organizing for a unit of this magnitude is enormous. Although the activity actually takes place in early June, the preparation for it begins during our team meetings in late February. At that time, the teacher in charge of the unit gets commitments from the other faculty members to plan and supervise the thirty-odd varied activities that constitute the unit. These activities have been designed so that every student, regardless of ability has a chance to succeed and earn a good grade. Some activities are required; some are elective. Some are especially suitable for high academic achievers; some are for athletes, artists, performers; while others appeal to those who do well in crafts, cooking, or sewing.

An eleven page booklet is prepared for the students. It includes everything they need to know about The Roaring Twenties project. Each activity is completely detailed and described, and the point values to be gained by successfully completing the various activities are included.

Students' grades for the I.D.U. depend upon the total points they accumulate by participating in many different activities. The final grade achieved is applied across the board for every basic class (Social Studies, Math, Language Arts, Science, and Reading). Extra credit points are earned if they participate in an activity connected to a related arts class.

Earning a good grade is admittedly a strong motivating factor for many students, but attendance during the week the unit culminates runs well above average indicating student interest and genuine involvement. It is a rare occasion that any student is absent for anything other than a very serious reason.

The required activities account for 70 points by themselves, and students can earn another 10 points by simply being part of a good audience. Most students seem to have little difficulty earning a *B*, and it is not uncommon for students to earn considerably more points than are required for an *A*. Failures rarely occur. Irrespective of grade, however, the educational and social benefits of participating in such a school-wide endeavor are substantial.

DESCRIPTION OF MAJOR ACTIVITIES

A. Required Activities

1. **Stock Market Demonstrations** (5 points) The day before the I.D.U. begins, every student participates in a demonstration about how to play the stock market. A quiz and clarifications are given at the end of the session. Students are given $5000.00 to begin playing.

2.   **Character Day** (Up to 30 points) During the fourth day of the I.D.U., every student dresses up as a character from the 1920s. They must research their person (5 points), make up a 5x8 name tag with pertinent facts (5 points), and dress up as the character (10 points). If they are one of the twenty-five winners at the fashion show at the end of the day, they earn 10 more points.

3.   **Portfolio** (5 points) Each student must keep a neatly organized portfolio that includes all transactions and activities participated in during the week. Failure to do so could result in 15 points being subtracted from the total.

4.   **Olympic Spectator** (5 points) The Roaring Twenties concludes with Olympic Games. For being well behaved, enthusiastic spectators, students earn 5 points.

B. **Required/Elective Activities**

1.   **BiJou** (Up to 30 points) Students must view at least four films (5 points each) from or about the 20s, and may see as many as six. Film summaries must be completed and included in the portfolio.

2.   **The 20s Book of Facts and Figures** (Up to 20 points) Students learn about and produce stories, word puzzles, posters, and examples of writing related to life in the 1920s. They must complete three assignments and may do four.

C. **Elective Activities**

1. **Time Line (5** points) Students may work in a group to construct and illustrate a mural sized time line depicting major events of the era.

2. **Banker** (25 points) Students who choose to do so are trained to be a teller in the bank.

3. **Bull Market Broker** (25 points) The Bull Market is where students buy their stocks. While all students participate in buying & selling stocks, training as a broker earns additional points.

4. **The Bear Market Broker** (25 points) The Bear Market is where stocks are sold. As above, training as a broker can yield additional points.

Grades are determined by points accumulated from participating in various activities.

5. **Investment Firm Broker** (25 points) This firm uses a computer-based math program that helps to predict market trends and provides investment opportunities.

6. **KDKA Radio Station** (20 points) Students write announcements and skits that are broadcast over the public address system twice daily.

7. **The Gazette Newspaper** (20 points) News articles, poems, puzzles, and interviews are published by the students two times a day.

8. **Cabaret** (30 points) A Roaring 20s speakeasy with dancers, singers, musicians, comedians, jugglers, and refreshments. Performances are given twice daily.

9. **Cabaret Spectator** (5 points) Points are given for being a courteous member of the audience.

10. **The Scopes Trial—Man or Ape** (25 points) Students research, produce, and perform on videotape a play based on some of the important issues dealing with the theory of evolution.

11 . **Scopes Trial Spectator** (5 points) Worksheets must be completed by the spectators at the end of the performance.

12. **Science Fair** (25 points) By constructing diagrams, models, illustrations, or projects students can demonstrate their understanding of the scientific advancements of the decade.

13. **Fashions and Foods** (Up to 20 points) Students can create illustrations of or actual fashions from the period; opportunities are provided to prepare the era's popular foods. Points are awarded according to the quality of the project.

14. **Olympic Village** (Up to 20 points) Flags, medals, uniforms, posters, programs, charts, maps, and reports can be made in the Olympic Village. The number of points earned depends upon the difficulty and quality of the work.

15. **Olympic Athlete** (10 points) The Olympics are held the last day of the I.D.U. Students participate in a variety of athletic activities, contests, and ceremonies that represent the Olympics of the 1920s. The winning Olympic athletes earn an additional 10 points.

Some of the activities listed above are ongoing and continuous, while others like the Cabaret, Bijou, The Book of Facts and Figures, and The Scopes Trial operate on very specific schedules. It is obvious that there must be meticulous organizational work done in order to maximize the opportunities for every student to participate fully.

Conclusion

I.D.U.s can be judged to be successful only when they are generated from the curriculum and faculty interest, and are enthusiastically received by the students. The Roaring Twenties is such a unit. It is monumental in both its preparation and execution, but well worth it. The activity provides a perfect blend of cognitive and affective education. Information acquired is substantial and demonstrates the wholeness of learning. The relationships between the 1920s and the present become evident. A feeling of camaraderie is generated among the faculty and student body that is invaluable. The unit is planned to coincide with the end of school. When it is over students and faculty are so drained from the excitement and emotion of the week that it would be difficult to gear up for another week of school. More importantly, all finish the year feeling good about themselves.

Since Upper Darby is a small community, it is a common occurrence for former students to run into faculty members. When that occurs the most frequent comment runs like this, "Are you still doing The Roaring Twenties? Boy, that was the best!" ▲

> This IDU provides a perfect blend of cognitive and affective education. It is a perfect way to conclude the year with enthusiasm.

When you understand all about the sun and all about the atmosphere and all about the rotation of the earth, you may still miss the radiance of the sunset.

— Alfred North Whitehead

What can be known, say, about Autumn can take form in scientific propositions that deal with chemical changes in trees, in astronomical propositions about the location of our planet in relation to the sun, in poetic expression disclosing the smell of burning autumn leaves, in visual images that present to our consciousness the color of a Vermont landscape, and in auditory forms that capture the crackle of leaves under our footsteps.

— Elliot Eisner

A FORMAT FOR INTERDISCIPLINARY INSTRUCTION

Theme	Make it broad enough to: • Encompass basic skills of reading, writing, computation, problem-solving, decision-making and creative thinking. • Be relevant to middle school students. • Last from three to ten days.
Title	Make it creative and fun!

Objectives	List at least two objectives for each subject area:
	    Language Arts, Social Studies,Math, Science,Music,
	    Art, Industrial Arts, and Physical Education

Glossary	Prepare a glossary of key terms, vocabulary, or concepts that are important to the mastery of the material.
Student Record Sheet	Develop a Table of Contents for each activity in the unit to serve as a record-keeping tool for the students.
Activities in Each Discipline	Use this format in preparing your activities including: Title, Objective, Materials Needed, Procedure, Evaluation.
Homework and/or Enrichment Ideas	Create a list of tasks that could be assigned as homework or enrichment for students.
Post-test/Project Presentation	Include a post-test and/or directions for a final project to serve as the evaluation for the unit in addition to those used as part of the activities.
Bibliography	List resources/references for follow-up or for later use.

Developed by Sandra Schurr, National Resource Center for Middle Grades Education.

Learning by Solving Real Problems

JOHN CARR, PETER EPPIG, PETER MONETHER

Every year several multi-grade, full-time, problem-centered, hands-on learning projects are carried out in this New Hampshire school.

An effective approach to learning by solving real problems can be found in the middle school in Peterborough, New Hampshire. Several times a year, three teachers and approximately seventy-five 6th, 7th and 8th grade students immerse themselves in a significant problem solving activity. This program, called *Interface*, began in the fall of 1982. It is based on "the fundamental principles of connectedness of things and motivation to learn (which) remain as significant today as when Dewey wrote (about) them" (Cawelti, 1984).

Peterborough's Interface Program

Interface is a WAY OF LEARNING by working within groups and using critical skills to solve real problems.

Critical skills are those involved in problem-solving, communication, decision-making, organization, management, independent learning, documentation, and cooperation, all of which are especially appropriate for middle school students.(For a complete list of these skills, see page 124.)

A real problem is defined here as one which interests students and has some degree of social significance. The breadth of the problem requires students to gather information from sources well beyond the classroom and the school. For example, in an effort to determine the ideal location for a proposed new site for their regional middle school, students met with or telephoned two architects, numerous realtors, the school district's director of buildings and grounds, and the owners of three buildings which might be renovated to become schools.

Some other problems which have been used for *Interface* include: determining the feasibility of heating a school with wood, designing a playground for a school which had none, and determining which international charitable organization would make the best use of donations.

Depending on the task, *Interface* sessions can last from a few days to two weeks. Teacher preparation, of course, begins well in advance. Determining the nature and scope of the problem, anticipating ways students will try to solve it, and notifying business and other community persons who might be approached by the students with questions are all part of the planning process.

It should also be noted that group decision making and problem solving techniques (critical skills), widely advocated for middle level students, are included in the regular school curriculum, so that students have had some opportunity to practice these skills prior to an *Interface* experience. *Interface* gives students an opportunity to use these processes intensively and also to decide which ones best suit particular circumstances.

Getting Started

Sometime during the week prior to *Interface,* the teachers notify the students in writing of the problem. For the purpose of this article, the challenge of publishing the fiftieth anniversary issue of an imaginary weekly news magazine, "Timeweek," in the year 2037, is used as the example. Once *Interface* begins, the regular classes, with the exception of art, music, physical education, industrial arts, and home economics are cancelled. This experience usually comes between marking periods. The entire academic day is devoted to the problem. Each day opens and closes with a general meeting. Students decided what work needs doing, who will do it, and how and when it will be done. For instance, at Timeweek's first morning session they decided on leaders for meetings, the best organizational format, and even assigned themselves homework — without prompting from teachers.

Student and Teacher Roles

It is important that students realize that the process, not just the product, is the focus, and to have faith that a good process will result in a good product. Students plan and carry out all the work, and as they grow in willingness to learn from mistakes, in independence in work, and in understanding that teachers are not convenient dispensers of knowledge upon request, the process becomes less frustrating and more meaningful to them.

Teachers act as resources, evaluators, and guides, but not directors. They challenge students without undue pressure, refrain from giving easy answers to student questions, and evaluate individual participation in a group process. They must know when and how to intervene when students are having problems that are not being resolved.

Evaluation

The process is evaluated by the teachers who observe the procedures used by the students to deal with problems. This formative analysis of the process is ongoing. Each day, teachers record comments and observations. This information is typed, duplicated, and distributed to all students and parents on a daily basis. Discussion of teacher feedback takes place during one or both of the general sessions. The following are selected teacher comments concerning Timeweek's first day:

Subjects, as such, are forgotten as solutions to real problems are sought.

Academic classes are suspended during *Interface* and the typical roles of students and teachers change dramatically.

122

- procedures and goals were not decided upon before the meeting started; was this a handicap?

- leaders at least for a while did a really fine job of distinguishing between identification of ideas and evaluative comments about them.

- there was a direct correlation between positive treatment of others and progress, negative treatment of others and stagnation.

Interface project results are evaluated by an independent panel. Panel members, selected by the teachers, are invited by students to convene on the last day of *Interface* for the purpose of judging the project. Usually judging panels are composed of other educators and persons who have some expertise in the problem being solved. Timeweek's review panel included editors of two local newspapers, the publisher of *Yankee Magazine,* a professional proofreader, the U.S. Congressman from the area, a prominent environmentalist, a school board member, and two other local business leaders. Each judge had been given a copy of Timeweek one week prior to the evaluation session. The summative evaluation of the judges showed consensus regarding a well-done product. The panel members pointed out, however, that a publication in the "real" world would have to be completely free of error. Timeweek was not. Insufficient research and inconsistencies were among the weaknesses mentioned.

At the end of each *Interface,* teachers give a "report card" to every student. This final evaluation is based on how well each student had been able to apply the critical skills listed on page 124.

The Value of *Interface*

In spite of inevitable frustration associated with a non-traditional process involving non-traditional roles, and a rather heavy workload for teachers, there are compelling answers to the question "Why bother?"

Quotes from students who took part in the Timeweek *Interface* help answer "why?"

BECAUSE a successful *Interface* will pose a problem that students want to solve, a problem that has many potential solutions and many ways to reach solutions. "It's fun to do things in your own way instead of the way someone else tells you to." In other words, the challenge of solving the problem is the main motivator, not pleasing the teacher or getting a good grade. In addition, because most *Interface* problems are solved through teamwork, there is the motivation of not wanting to let the others down. "We had to communicate in order to work together." "We learn cooperation. We had to work together and sometimes that was hard."

An independent panel of evaluators judge the project.

CRITICAL SKILLS

Problem-solving skills

1. Identifies parameters of the problem before solving
2. Makes justifiable assumptions about the problem
3. Gathers a wide range of relevant information
4. Analyzes/weighs information gathered
5. Uses relevant information and concepts to solve problems
6. Considers more than one solution
7. Solves problem based on its definition
8. Tests possible solutions to the problem

Communication skills

1. Communicates well orally to groups and one-on-one
2. Communicates well in writing: clear, concise, organized
3. Communicates well graphically: neat, clear, complete

Decision-making skills

1. Is able to make decisions on important or relevant issues.
2. Is willing and able to compromise at appropriate times
3. Uses consensus of ideas for group decision-making
4. Is able to provide rationale for decisions
5. Is aware of consequences of decisions.

Organization skills

1. Budgets time well
2. Organizes and files appropriate information
3. Effectively creates and utilizes a working area
4. Prepares and plans effectively
5. Concentrates and perseveres on given tasks

Management skills

1. Keeps informed of group and overall progress
2. Facilitates group functioning
3. Keeps people on task
4. Provides leadership for group or overall organization
5. Effectively participates in meetings

Independent learning skills

1. Works well on one's own without outside direction
2. Takes initiative in assigning self-additional tasks
3. Is aware of and utilizes appropriate sources

Documentation skills

1. Takes notes at small and large group meetings
2. Makes good contributions to the writing of daily logs
3. Keeps copies of important documents
4. Compiles daily agendas for following day's work

Cooperation skills

1. Cooperates with group members
2. Cooperates with other groups
3. Uses tact and diplomacy to solicit information or make requests.

BECAUSE, ideally, throughout this problem-solving process, students are connected with the real world. For example, Timeweek magazine was the students' very own product, and the process leading to its publication was akin to that of a real publishing company. Students had researched several area publishers for organizational ideas. "The process was important. Without a process that worked, we wouldn't have had a product."

BECAUSE, as students develop skills, their self-confidence grows. "We found out we could do a half-decent job in two weeks."

BECAUSE *Interface* is planned to provide a safe environment where students learn from failure as well as from success. "A positive attitude leads to a positive attitude. When something went well, more things went well. That makes me think if we keep trying to be positive maybe we can keep from having nuclear war."

BECAUSE artificial barriers between disciplines are removed. "School subjects like math and science were all a part of what we had to do only we didn't have them like separate courses. It was more interesting this way."

BECAUSE of necessity the student becomes a more active participant in learning — the phrase "learning by doing" fits. "We learned to be independent. If we asked the teachers questions, instead of giving us answers, they asked us another question." "We learned to use resources other than books." "We learned to solve problems because we kept having to solve problems in everything we did."

And BECAUSE *Interface* fosters a sense of community among students, a common purpose exists.

Concluding Comments

The value of learning by solving real problems lies in two key characteristics: the ability to motivate students to learn and the absence of artificial barriers among curricular areas. Moreover, because students develop problem-solving skills, its utility can be lifelong. Learning must not stop at the level of factual acquisition. Information must be analyzed, evaluated, applied, and, above all, synthesized. Learning by solving real problems encourages student ideas, and "...regardless of what some advertisers have led us to believe, this country does not run on oil. It runs on ideas" (Kane, 1981).

When students are allowed, even urged, to question, to seek answers to those questions, and to defend their answers and ideas to impartial judges, the individual, and society as well, benefits. ▲

"School subjects like math and science were all a part of what we had to do only we didn't have them like separate courses. It was more interesting this way."

References

Cawelti, Gordon, *ASCD Update,* p. 2, September, 1984.

Kane, Carolyn *Newsweek,* December 24, 1981.

Goals for Personal Development As Team Member

This form will help you think about your relationships with others and your skills in teamwork. It also will give you a chance to set your own goals for development.

1. Read through the list and decide which items you are doing all right on, which ones you should do more often, and which ones you should do less often. Mark each item in the appropriate column.
2. Some aspects of group interaction that are not listed may be more important to you than those listed. Write in such aspects on the blank lines.

	Doing all right	Need to do it more	Need to do it less
Communications Skills			
1. Talking in the group			
2. Being brief and concise			
3 Being forceful			
4. Drawing others out			
5. Listening alertly			
6. Thinking before I talk			
7. Keeping my remarks on the topic			
8._____			
Observation Skills			
1. Noting tension in group			
2. Noting who talks to whom			
3. Noting interest level of group			
4. Sensing feelings of individuals			
5. Noting who is being "left out."			
6. Noting reactions to my comments			
7. Noting when group avoids a topic.			
8. _____			
Morale-building Skills			
1. Showing interest			
2. Working to keep people from being ignored			
3. Harmonizing, helping people reach agreement			
4. Reducing tension			
5. Upholding rights of individuals in the face of group pressure			
6. Expressing praise or appreciation			
7. _____			

GOALS (continued)	Doing all right	Need to do it more	Need to do it less

Problem-solving Skills
1. Stating problems or goals
2. Asking for ideas, opinions
3. Giving ideas, opinions
4. Evaluating ideas critically
5. Summarizing discussions
6. Clarifying issues
7. _____

Emotional Expressiveness
1. Telling others what I feel.
2. Hiding my emotions
3. Disagreeing openly
4. Expressing warm feelings
5. Expressing gratitude
6. Being sarcastic
7. _____

Ability to Face and Accept Emotional Situations
1. Being able to face conflict, anger
2. Being able to face closeness, affection
3. Being able to face disappointment
4. Being able to stand silence
5. Being able to stand tension
6. _____

Social Relationships
1. Competing to outdo others
2. Acting dominant toward others
3. Trusting others
4. Being helpful
5. Being protective
6. Calling attention to myself
7. Being able to stand up for myself.
8. _____

General
1. Understanding why I do what I do
2. Encouraging comments on my own behavior (feedback)
3. Accepting help willingly
4. Making my mind up firmly
5. Criticizing myself
6. Waiting patiently
7. Going off by myself to read or think
8. _____

Source: Rene Pino and Ruth Emory, National Regional Educational Laboratory, Portland, Oregon, 1975.

Traps To Avoid

1. Failing to recognize that team organization is fundamentally different from traditional departmentalized or self-contained arrangements.

2. Attempting to team without adequate staff development in such aspects as team skills (communications, group decision-making, and organization of effective meetings) and team practices (goal setting, record keeping, evaluation).

3. Failing to place team organization at the top of the scheduling priority list so that all else revolves around it — and not the other way around.

4. Failing to understand that new teams will need time and practice in order to develop into fully functioning teams.

5. Failing to consider personalities and interpersonal variables when staffing teaching teams and planning for staff development.

6. Attempting to team without choosing somebody to be responsible for the ongoing monitoring and support of teaming, which must include regular communication between teamed teachers and administrators.

7. Failing to organize teams so that they are comprised of teachers with a common planning period who teach different core subjects to a common group of students in some common area of the building.

8. Failing to understand the significance of team identify and the power of symbols, ritual, and ceremony in the life of the team.

9. Failing to integrate team organization with the rest of the school program.

10. Failing to nurture faculty esprit de corps, and failing to nurture academic departments, which retain some important functions.

11. Failing to set goals for the growth and development of teams.

Erb, Thomas O. and Doda, Nancy M., *Team Organization: Promise, Practices and Possibilities* (1989) Washington, DC: National Education Association, pp. 116-122. Used with permission.

WATERSHED: At the Confluence of Curricula

Mark Springer

A truly remarkable year-long, all day, every day fully integrated experiential seventh grade curriculum.

Watershed means learning. Throughout the year my head was crammed with many little bits of information. Each bit had importance and they all tied together. That's what was different. The things we learned were important, and we would remember them.

With these words, Lynette Winters captured the essence of Radnor Middle School's WATERSHED program on the closing day of her seventh grade year. Twelve months earlier, Lynette, and thirty-seven of her peers representing the spectrum of ability levels, elected to pass up the normal seventh grade curriculum of separate math, English, science, and history classes. She declined the opportunity to take unconnected courses in art, music, home economics or technical education. She even gave up gym class. She voluntarily put aside the comfortable but limiting confines of all these traditional curricula.

Instead, Lynette opted to spend her seventh grade in one room — all day, every day; studying one subject — local streams. She chose to participate in WATERSHED, Radnor's alternative seventh grade program which gives students like Lynette a chance to take control of their learning. Employing cooperative learning and discovery strategies, the WATERSHED program helps students see their learning as part of an integrated whole. Traditional curricular barriers are removed to allow a re-unification of concepts and skills under three broader perspectives: a *Sense of Place*, a *Sense of Time*, and a *Sense of Quality*.

The first of these perspectives focuses on the physical parameters which constitute a stream and its drainage area. Lynette, for example, studied the geology, the geomorphology, and the climate of our area. She learned about the hydrologic, the carbon-oxygen, and the nitrogen cycles. She acquainted herself with the region's plants and animals and with the food/energy webs which bind them together. At one point Lynette became an insect of the water's surface to write about a day in her life. Another time she was a drop of water experiencing the water cycle and adventuring down the stream.

Throughout this first portion of our study Lynette developed many mapping skills. She located our streams in relation to the nation, the state, and the region. She drew maps illustrating the geological aspects of the watershed, which she then related to bottom and gradient profiles she made. Using U.S.G.S. 7.5 minute maps as a resource, Lynette constructed to scale a three-dimensional topographic map of the watershed.

Even the best map, however, cannot compare with first-hand experience of a landscape. So, Lynette and her classmates spent many days exploring the watershed in person. By bus and van, we toured the watershed from headwaters to mouth, and we walked long stretches of the stream. On these field study trips the students took photographs, sketched scenes, and wrote descriptions and poetry. They tested the stream for dissolved oxygen and carbon dioxide, pH, and nitrates. They measured and recorded the width, average depth and velocity, and they calculated a flow. They also calculated a biotic index of benthic invertebrates based on several sampling techniques. After each trip the students interpreted the data they had gathered, and they wrote about their experiences.

Students face new challenges and confront real problems and issues.

As colder weather began to preclude regular field testing, Lynette and her classmates turned their attention to the second focus of our year. Our *Sense of Time* perspective examines the interrelationships between the streams and the people who have inhabited the region over time. Lynette gathered primary source information about the pre-Columbian native Leni-Lenape and about the subsequent groups of European settlers who colonized our region. She analyzed the important role our streams played in the American Revolution. She traced human interaction with the streams through the rise of agriculture, milling and other industries; and she surveyed the effects on our streams of massive immigration and westward expansion during the nineteenth and early twentieth centuries.

Trips through the winter included visits to museums and historical sites. Among other experiences, Lynette spent a day as a Lenape, stood on the rocks where the first Swedish settlers landed, shivered on a redoubt at Valley Forge in January, and felt the cool spray from waterwheels in grist mills and black powder mills. Back at school Lynette used information she gathered to create a colony of her own, to write American Diaries, to construct a colonial artifact, to publish a newspaper, and to debate issues which affected our area during the Revolutionary and Civil wars.

With spring and the return of good field testing weather, the emphasis shifts to a *Sense of Quality*. The students applied what they had learned about the physical and historical conditions of the water shed to an investigation of contemporary conditions.

Along with the new round of field testing trips, Lynette studied and mapped the systems of the human body. This led to an examination of similar systems as they exist on a larger, societal scale. For example, Lynette compared the parts and systems of her body to those of her house. She mapped these house systems by designing the floor plans and constructing a model of her dream house. Then Lynette studied parallel water and waste-water treatment processes, as well as transportation, energy, and regulatory systems in the region. In each case, visits to functioning facilities helped Lynette and her group prepare their final evaluation of the overall quality of our watersheds today and in the future.

By year's end, Lynette had seen our local watersheds as unique environments and integral parts of a larger whole. She had learned about the intricate relationships that tie us to our watersheds and how our actions now and in the future directly affect the quality of life.

While examining these relationships Lynette mastered most of the same information covered in the traditional program and much more. The eighth grade teachers report that WATERSHED students in general tend to be confident, enthusiastic and well-prepared for the materials covered in Radnor's eighth grade curriculum. Checking standardized test scores over the five years we find that the two hundred or so WATERSHED students, including Lynette, scored just as well on these tests as did students in traditional classes.

WATERSHED students handle the eighth grade curriculum in good fashion — and score well on tests.

The most notable difference between WATERSHED students and their peers shows up in their respective writing skills. Every year WATERSHED students as a group show a significantly greater degree of improvement in their ability to write cogently and creatively. At least in part this can be attributed to the WATERSHED program's structure. Because WATERSHED has a limited number of students for a virtually unlimited amount of time, and because WATERSHED does not arbitrarily divide time into forty or fifty minute periods devoted to segregated subject areas, writing is emphasized as a continual process, and the students have the chance to explore fully the writing process in a variety of forms.

WATERSHED students show significant improvement in their writing ability.

Just as important, the integrated nature of the program also helps students improve their writing. Writing assignments grow directly out of first-hand experiences. This gives added meaning to the writing process, as students see a personal value in their writing. Furthermore, since all the experiences and activities which form the subjects of writing tasks relate to one another, each writing assignment has a contextual significance which students can grasp and appreciate. Instead of a dull chore, writing becomes an enjoyable process, a personalized extension of each student's experience. When polled at the close of each year, WATERSHED students cite with pride the changes seen in their writing and in their attitudes toward writing.

Overall, students, teachers, and parents agree that the WATER-SHED experience is remarkably successful. The students, including Lynette, improve their skills in writing, reading, research and public speaking. They face new challenges and confront real world problems and issues. Along the way they see many parallels between themselves and a watershed. For example, while Lynette retained and strengthened her individuality and self-esteem, she also played an important part in the successful functioning of the whole group. Through her adherence to WATERSHED's "Five C's" of Commitment, Cooperation, Caring, Caution, and Courage, Lynette made the year a successful learning experience for everyone involved.

Finally, Lynette and her classmates had the chance to learn that subject areas as presented in traditional curricula are not in themselves as important as their interrelationship and their application to real life. The students, most for the first time, had the chance to see learning as a confluence of information and ideas. Dylan Bank, one of Lynette's classmates this past year, summed up his WATERSHED experience this way:

I consider myself one of the lucky ones. I got a chance to work on photography; I loved it. I got a chance to work on my writing; I loved it. I got a chance to get away from the normal schooling system; I loved it. I got a chance to make new friends; I loved it. I got a chance to look at the world in a different way; I loved it. I got a chance. ▲

The WATERSHED Program was developed and is taught by Mark Springer, Ed Silcox, and Woody Arnold at the Radnor Middle School in Wayne, Pennsylvania, 19807. They welcome inquiries and can be reached at the school address or by phone at (215) 688-8100 ext. 271.

From Whitehead's *The Aims of Education,* 1929

The solution which I am urging is to eradicate the fatal disconnection of subjects which kills the vitality of our modern curriculum. You may not divide the seamless cloak of learning. There is only one subject matter for education, and that is Life in all its manifestations. Instead of this single unity, we offer children — algebra, from which nothing follows; geometry, from which nothing follows; science, from which nothing follows; history, from which nothing follows; a couple of languages, never mastered; and lastly, most dreary of all, literature, represented by plays of Shakespeare with ... substance to be committed to memory. Can such a list be said to represent Life, as it is known in the midst of the living of it? The best that can be said of it is, that it is a rapid table of contents which a deity might run over in his mind while he was thinking of creating a world, and had not yet determined how to put together.

SECTION IV

Nurturing Teaming and Guiding Growth

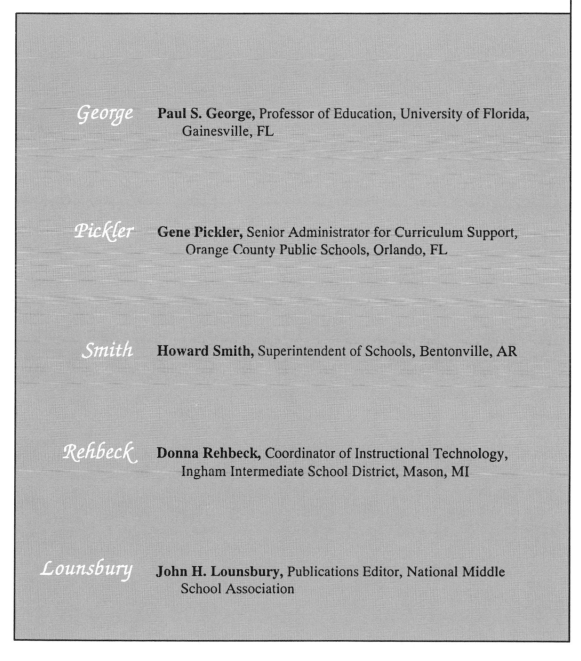

George   **Paul S. George,** Professor of Education, University of Florida, Gainesville, FL

Pickler   **Gene Pickler,** Senior Administrator for Curriculum Support, Orange County Public Schools, Orlando, FL

Smith   **Howard Smith,** Superintendent of Schools, Bentonville, AR

Rehbeck   **Donna Rehbeck,** Coordinator of Instructional Technology, Ingham Intermediate School District, Mason, MI

Lounsbury   **John H. Lounsbury,** Publications Editor, National Middle School Association

Four Phases in the Life of a Team

PAUL S. GEORGE

The four operational stages in the life of interdisciplinary teams are important to understanding and achieving their full development.

In the past three decades, thousands of educators in middle level schools have opted to organize teachers and students into interdisciplinary teams. We know why. We know how. What has not been so obvious until now, perhaps because it seems so contradictory, is that the interdisciplinary team organization, as an educational arrangement of teachers and students, is both remarkably variable and dramatically uniform, at once. Understanding this seemingly ironic situation is essential to the long term success and survival of this apparently effective organizational strategy.

In over twenty years this writer has had the special opportunity to spend a significant portion of time as a participant-observer in well over 300 middle and junior high schools, as educators in the schools struggled with the task of organizing teachers and students for instruction. In every case, the schools were being organized around the concept of the interdisciplinary team, either as a new school plan or as part of the conversion of the school from a junior high to a middle school. There appears to be a series of four stages or phases in the life of a fully-functioning interdisciplinary team.

As in other areas of the process of reorganization to middle school, these phases appear at different times and take different forms, depending on the context in which the interdisciplinary team is introduced That is, when a middle school results from the reorganization of a junior high school, with the same building and staff, the functions of the team seem to unfold as a series of stages or phases, one after the other. In other situations, however, where the middle school comes as a result of a combination of the staffs of several preexisting schools, in a plant where a large portion of the faculty has no established pattern of behavior, these functions all seem to emerge simultaneously, but only in partially complete form. What follows is a description of what the author perceives to be the ways in which the team organization evolves in both contexts, and with some suggestions for effective administrative responses to this phenomenon.

Phase One: Organization

Regardless of the school setting in which the team is found, the first phase of life for the team is always an organizational one. An authentic interdisciplinary team organization does not exist, in this writer's opinion, unless several critical conditions are met: teachers and students on the team are located together in the same area of the school; teachers share the same schedule, at least roughly; and, there are at least two, usually more, subjects taught to the students on the team by the same combination of teachers involved. When these conditions exist, the life of the team begins; when they do not, the future of the team is limited by the degree to which the conditions are absent.

Once these requirements have been satisfied, either with or without the participation of the teachers in the decision, the team begins to jell. Students notice that they are in classes with others who have the same teachers at the same or different times during the day. The students observe that they do not travel as widely from one part of the building to another as frequently as they may have under prior arrangements. Teachers, students say, begin to unite in their academic and behavioral expectations of students. Even if they have not been told by the teachers of the existence of the team, students will begin to feel its effects.

Teachers, too, respond to the new conditions. Opportunities for improving their classroom experiences present themselves, and teachers take advantage of the new organization in several ways. Almost immediately, the teachers on the team realize the power inherent in their acting together. Team rules for student behavior, usually a bit different from school rules, appear and are supported by each individual teacher in a way that brings increasing awareness and compliance from students. Time between classes is more closely supervised. Common processes, such as a heading for papers, make an obvious improvement in the ability of the students to follow directions. Team conferences with parents and administrators are less intimidating and more productive. Teachers almost always report that their jobs are more satisfying and more productive.

Phase Two: Community

Once organized and operating somewhat in concert, teachers and students become more aware of their new arrangement and a sense of community becomes possible. The experience of many middle and junior high school educators is that both teachers and students yearn for this group identity; but while some degree of group feeling results naturally, from the existence of the organization, a really satisfying sense of community must be nurtured. The need must be recognized, goals set for its realization, and activities conducted with commitment. This affective component of the team organization can be powerfully productive.

For teachers, the sense of community can be the redeeming virtue of the team organization. This writer has, countless times, encountered veteran educators who spoke of the team arrangement as the factor that enabled them to continue teaching, with a sense of joy and commitment that had long been absent from their lives in school.

To have a real team requires common students, common schedule, and common space.

Teachers readily realize the power inherent in acting together.

A really satisfying sense of community must be nurtured.

Statements like, "I've taught for 27 years in this school, and this year has been the best of them all," are not uncommon.

Teachers who are confronted with a career that is as disappointing as it is unavoidable tend to withdraw, psychologically, from the life of the school. Their commitments, extra efforts, hopes, and enthusiasm go elsewhere: to their church, their sports, family, avocation, or illness. They put in their days, but their hearts are absent. These same teachers, who are naturally skeptical of the initial effort to reorganize, sometimes develop into its strongest supporters when they experience the rewards of working together with other teachers. Faculty morale almost always increases, often dramatically, as the sense of community develops among the team of teachers. Few teachers really prefer to live and work in complete isolation from their peers.

Students, of course, require this sense of community even more than the faculty. The experience of the last decade, supported by considerable research in the area of human development, suggests that early adolescent students need smaller groups of teachers and students with which to identify than the traditionally organized junior high school permits. Instead of a school of 1500, a team of 150 is much more manageable for the early adolescent. The team offers a turf to belong on and a group to join. Teachers alert to the need for this sense of community in their students can make a major difference in the level of group feeling that exists in the team.

Faculties who are interested in increasing this feeling often rely on a variety of very similar devices. Team names, colors, mottos, songs, T-shirts, and other visibly common possessions help to heighten the sense of community. Contests, special meals, meetings, field trips and a host of other activities in which students and teachers on a team can engage together tighten the bonds of team feeling. Interdisciplinary curriculum units involving the whole team also facilitate the continued development of the group sense. Some schools, new and old, go so far as to paint or carpet the team areas in different hues, furthering the objective of team feeling. However it is accomplished, intentionally enhancing the team's sense of community is critical to the emergence of this phase of team organization.

Parents, too, can participate in and benefit from the sense of community that the team organization yields. A memo or newsletter sent home can inform parents about the existence of the team. Team-parent conferences can demonstrate the effectiveness of a combined effort. Team get-togethers that include parents develop and broaden the base of support for the team concept, and pot-luck dinners and team presentations can bring parents to school in ways that are very satisfying to everyone. Few schools that involve parents this way find parental criticism of the school to be a serious concern.

Phase Three: Teamed Instruction

Teams that are well-organized and that have a sense of who they are, when possessing several additional characteristics, are able to enter the third phase of team life. Teamed instruction is that phase of interdisciplinary team life most often taken, mistakenly, as the whole. That is, for many years team organization and team teaching were thought of, by many educators, as being totally synonymous. The argument presented here is that actual team teaching is only one part of the interdisciplinary plan, one that emerges only under certain conditions. And, while team teaching is often desirable, even when it is absent, team organization is still extremely worthwhile. Teamed instruction is an important part of, but not all there is to, the interdisciplinary team organization.

The success of team teaching efforts is affected, not only by the team's passage through the first two phases, but by several other factors. Interdisciplinary team organization requires a great deal of planning time; and often, when this time is limited, there is little left to be used in planning actual efforts at collaboration in the classroom. Team teaching also demands, from teachers, the kinds of communication skills that only the more sophisticated educators possess. Furthermore, teamwork in the area of curriculum and instruction demands an entirely different set of planning skills than are required for individual teaching situations. When, however, there is adequate time, interest and planning skill present among the members of the team, actual team teaching may take several forms.

Initially, teachers on a team may find that simple attempts at collaboration are successful. Toward the end of the first year of team life, as a consequence of their discussions while in earlier phases, the teachers may have discovered that there were a significant number of occasions when each was teaching a set of objectives or topics that complemented the other. Prior to this discovery, teaming will have been limited to occasional agreements to coordinate the planning of field trips, exams, and other major efforts. At this point, however, the team's teachers will often make a serious effort to go further in their coordination of the curriculum in the year to come. They will attempt to manipulate their individual plans so that topics that match, although they are in different subjects, will be taught at the same time. When, for example, English literature is being taught in language arts, the social studies teacher will plan a unit on English history. There may even be a few joint assignments.

On teams where this effort at coordination happens effectively and teachers are stimulated by the experience, team teaching may

Teamed instruction is an important part of, but not all there is to, teaming.

enter a new area. Authentic interdisciplinary units may be taught by teachers who find themselves with the planning time required and congenial people with which to work. Units that tie together two, three, or four of the subjects taught by teachers on the team can be exciting for everyone. One team known to the author planned and taught a unit in which each team member contributed, from the perspective of his own area, a series of objectives within the general theme of "Bridges." Language arts focused on the bridge in literature, social studies on bridges in history and locally known structures, while the science teacher concentrated on the physics of bridges, and the math teacher used the time to design word problems on the same topic. Hundreds of such interdisciplinary units are taught on teams in American middle schools in any one year. Rarely, however, are the conditions so favorable that a team can manage to offer more than two or three such units to their students within any one academic year. The cost, in teacher effort, is simply too high.

For many educators this is the summit of the interdisciplinary effort, but experience seems to indicate that this is not always the end. One additional phase remains possible, for some teams.

Phase Four: Governmental

Fully-functioning teams arrive at the point where everyone involved, including the school administration, realizes that the organization and operation of a complete, complex middle school is far too difficult to be handled unilaterally by one or two people in the front office. Even if this were possible, it would not be preferable. Power sharing and group policy-making are both the process and the product of the interdisciplinary team organization.

Research and experience in the area of team organization indicate that teachers who successfully negotiate the first three phases of team life frequently find themselves motivated to assume more responsibility, professionally, for the decisions that affect their lives and the school experiences of their students. Teachers who work together and who jointly explore new dimensions of professional effort become aware of the complexity of the process of school management and, concomitantly, of the desirability of shared problem-solving and decision-making. It seems inevitable. Administrators who recognize the wisdom of a combined democratic executive approach to leadership, and who posses the ego strength to implement it, help teams grow toward these true limits of effectiveness.

Teachers, in such situations, usually take part in some form of representative government system. Often each team has a leader who represents the other teachers at weekly meetings of the Program Improvement Council, or a group by some other name constituted to

Power sharing and group policy-making are both the process and the product of the interdisciplinary team organization.

set policy and implement decisions in as democratic a manner as is possible, given the conditions of the particular school. One school, like many known to the author, builds the group from one teacher on each team, a representative of the unified arts and physical education faculty, a media specialist, counselor, and two members of the school administration. The group meets biweekly, on Monday afternoons. Team meetings are held the following Tuesday morning, and school faculty meetings on Tuesday afternoons on a biweekly basis. Therefore data are fresh and the decisions more informed.

When the situation is right, teams find themselves, through their representatives and at meetings of the total faculty, involved in a variety of discussions and decisions. Wise administrators, knowing the difference between decisions that can be shared and those that cannot, share as much decision-making power as possible. This is done, not condescendingly or patronizingly, but because schools run much more smoothly when teachers contribute authentically to the effort to make and implement important decisions.

Several areas of school policy seem particularly appropriate for this kind of democratic deliberation. One such item, consuming a great deal of time and attention in schools where teams have entered phase four, is the master schedule. Often the Council will identify and give power to a scheduling committee that will bring proposed models back to the Council for approval. Under these circumstances, of course, teams have wide latitude to manipulate their own team schedules and the individual schedules of students on the team. In fact, in these schools, one rarely finds students' schedules changed arbitrarily by someone in the front office. The teachers on the team are recognized, rightly, as having a great deal to say about how time is organized, for the team and the school. Usually a far better schedule results from this process than in those schools where the principal closets himself in the office for the summer and announces the new schedule to the teachers at the first faculty meeting in August, as though schedules came forth fully-formed, like Athena, from the forehead of Zeus.

In this phase, teachers on the team become involved in the decisions to promote or retain individual students as well as helping to determine the promotion-retention policy for the school as a whole. Students are treated as individuals and policies are drawn up that permit such flexibility. Nothing seems cut in stone.

Frequently, when teams are in the fourth phase, the budget is a subject of shared decision-making. The priorities for the expenditure of funds are not the exclusive province of the principal. Teachers help to decide whether monies should, for example, go toward the pur-

Often, team leaders become a part of a major policy-making body.

Schools run much more smoothly when teachers contribute authentically to important decisions.

140

chase of a new computer system or for an additional faculty member. Teams are given a portion of the school funds to use as a team budget (e.g., $10 per student, amounting to about $1500 on a team with 150 students), permitting them to make their own decisions about minor purchases and allocations that do not affect other teams.

Under these circumstances, team members learn that there are decisions that they have little interest in making (e.g., janitorial supplies), decisions that they cannot make (e.g., faculty evaluations), and many that they must participate in making. The autonomy of the school principal and his prerogatives are safeguarded by these understandings and conflict usually remains at a minimum, with teacher morale often at its highest levels. These are truly fully-functioning teams, helping to refine and implement school policy in ways that go a long way toward guaranteeing effective operation of the total program.

Administrative Responses to Phase Development

The role of the school administrator in relationship to the interdisciplinary team organization, as it develops through various phases, is complex and crucial. The principal can facilitate or frustrate the growth of the team, depending on whether he or she understands the phases through which teams grow, whether these phases are encouraged or resisted, and whether the principal has enough of a sense of self to be stimulated rather than threatened by these developments in the school. Principals seeking to help teams grow and function effectively should keep several strategies in mind.

It is, of course, extremely important for the school administrator to recognize the existence of these separate areas of team life, and to know that they emerge differently depending on whether the school is a new entity or is in transition from one organization to another. In the new middle school, each phase must be nurtured more nearly simultaneously, with an emphasis on the first and fourth phases in the early part of the new school's life. In the reorganized junior high school the principal must help establish the effectiveness of the teams in each phase as it appears, and encourage the teams to reach toward the next phase as they achieve success at a prior level.

The principal must precipitate the teams into just-manageable difficulty. That is, each team must be asked to perform the tasks demanded at each phase, and to move toward functioning in another area. Teams that are struggling to organize themselves, or to establish a sense of community, should not be asked to initiate sophisticated team teaching enterprises. The interdisciplinary organization can be damaged, as can any organism or institution, by being asked to perform functions for which it is not yet ready.

> **The principal can facilitate, or frustrate the growth of a team.**

The principal can help teams function effectively by making his expectations clear and by suggesting ways in which the team can meet those expectations. Team tasks can be spelled out at the beginning of the year; a team evaluation, in addition to those of each teacher, at the end of the year can assist the team in determining whether it is meeting the goals that have been established and what its members can do to grow toward being more effective and fully functioning as a group.

The interdisciplinary team organization is far more complex and considerably more variable than educators once believed. Fortunately, it also appears to be a more effective and a somewhat hardier variety of educational innovation than might have been expected. The number of schools organized into interdisciplinary teams has probably now moved beyond the 5,000 mark, spurred on by increasing numbers of junior high schools that are changing from department to team as the way in which teachers and students are organized for instruction. Most experienced administrators appear to regard the team as a part of the educational mainstream, certainly as a viable alternative, if not the preferred strategy. As educators learn more about the structure and function of the various phases of team organization, and how to facilitate them, the interdisciplinary team concept seems even more certain to become a permanent component of educational practice in the middle grades. Change in American education, permanent change for the better, may really be possible. ▲

Integrated Approaches Pass Accountability Muster

More than 70 studies have been carried out comparing student achievement in block-time, core, and interdisciplinary team programs with students in more conventional programs. In nearly every case, students in these innovative programs do as well as or better than their comparison groups. More than 15 normative studies give similar results, with students in experimental programs meeting or exceeding norms derived from administering standardized tests to students in conventional programs.

— Vars, Gordon, 1991. *A bibliography of research on the effectiveness of block-time, core, and interdisciplinary team teaching programs.* Kent, OH: National Association for Core Curriculum.

The Evolutionary Development of Interdisciplinary Teams

GENE PICKLER

Observation of actual teams reveals several stages of developmental progression described in these illustrations.

Interdisciplinary teaming is a seductive concept. It affords us the opportunity to bring into play the human relations, planning, organizational, and innovative instructional expertise that we all know we possess, but that has been suppressed by "the system."

However, the autonomy inherent in such an organizational structure may also permit some of our less desirable traits to surface. For the first time, many may come to realize that "the system" has been a convenient scapegoat for supporting their own preferred work styles. This should not be attributed to a basic flaw in human nature. It is more likely the result of a lack of practice in using skills beyond those that are required for working independently.

The literature that deals with interdisciplinary teaming is enticing. It is consistent with theories on productive work climates, employee satisfaction, and effectiveness. There is even support for the concept in recent national studies which advocate humanizing the institutional school setting and revitalizing the profession through increased teacher collaboration.

However, those who become enamored with the prospective benefits of teaming with-out also considering the human implications, do so at some peril. Teaming alters not only the roles of teachers but also their working environment.

The developmental progression illustrated on the next page is not theoretical. It is based upon the observation of actual teams in different settings at different levels of implementation. It is presented with the hope that those who are in the process of establishing teams will find comfort in the knowledge that some degree of initial floundering actually does represent a step toward effective teaming.

The delineations are not rigid. A team may find that some items from several stages are descriptive of its efforts. However, the stages do reflect a succession that teams usually experience.

Considerable benefits accrue when effective teaming strategies are employed. Making the transition from working in isolation to planning and acting in concert with others, however, requires commitment, time, and effort. A review of the descriptors can be helpful to practitioners in assessing progress toward developing their individual potential and the concept of teaming.

STAGE 1

We don't know each others' first names.
But, that's O.K. because we don't meet together anyway.
To be perfectly honest, we don't see any advantages or benefits to teaming.

STAGE 2

We meet occasionally.
We meet together for parent conferences mainly—
but we do not prepare for the conferences as a team.
When we do meet, our sessions often turn into gripe sessions.
Some of us would like to do more as a team—
others are less enthusiastic or downright negative about the idea.

STAGE 3

We get along pretty well with each other.
We meet pretty often—but not on a regular basis.
We have agreed upon a uniform set of team rules and procedures.
We try to coordinate our test dates, homework assignments.
We meet together prior to attending a parent conference.
We try to plan for the conference.

STAGE 4

We get along well. We generally like and respect each other.
We meet regularly. Our meetings are structured, purposeful, productive.
We have agreed upon a common set of team procedures for our students.
We have a team calendar so that we can coordinate tests, major projects.
This is posted in our classrooms so that our students can see it.
We share student information and look for strategies to deal with problems.
We have implemented some positive reinforcement strategies on our team.
We plan our parent conferences in advance and have suggestions ready.
We have worked on establishing a sense of team identity for our students.
We sometimes correlate our instruction when our content areas overlap.
We sometimes eat lunch together at school.

STAGE 5

We are truly a team. We cooperate with and support each other.
We have established a team identity for our students.
We bring all our students together for occasional activities.
Our team meetings are regularly scheduled. We follow an agenda. We
follow up on decisions that are made at our meetings.
We divide up the work that is to be done.
Our calendar is posted where our students can see it.
We share student information and concerns and look for team solutions to
problems. We also share information for the purpose of recognizing those
students who are doing well.
We have established some team goals for the year.
We plan reinforcement activities between subject areas when desirable.
We also reinforce basic skills as a team effort.
We meet with students to discuss problems or provide reinforcement.
We plan two or three thematic units during the year.
Our parent conferences are well planned, productive, and positive.
We plan some occasional "off the wall" activities for our students.
We often eat together at school—and sometimes even on workdays. ▲

A Guide for Assessing
the Development of Teaming

HOWARD W. SMITH

The author, sensing the need for clarifying expectations, created a chart which would permit teams to assess formally their development.

A major emphasis in the development of teaming is pre-planning and pre-organization. Many times concentration is on end results with a tendency not to do as much advance planning and as much pre-staging of information for teachers as necessary. Educators talk about anticipatory set for instructional effectiveness or setting the stage for learning. Development of teaming has a need for setting the stage so teachers may progress through development in a sequential fashion.

During development of teaming expectations should be set to focus teachers toward teaming outcomes. Like most collaborative small group processes, particular teaming concepts develop over time. Pickler (1987) (see p.144) identified this concept as well through his evolution of interdisciplinary teams which show five stages that teams evolve through. This concept of development over time has led me to formulate a timeline of expectations for teaming over a three year period (page 147).

Set Expectations

During pre-planning, set major expectations for teaming. Critical to understanding teaming is the development of clear expectations which clarify its functions. Merenbloom (1988) states, "Teams of teachers should be given structure for the function of a team." Focus teaming by listing what is expected to be accomplished. The Teaming Expectations Guide (Figure 1), provides guidance in structure and functions. The idea of focus and careful planning is widely supported. Interdisciplinary teaming does not just happen, but must be carefully planned. The Teaming Expectations Guide sets focus and structure for teaming from which further expectations can be clarified.

Maximize Ownership

Secondly, teaming needs the full support of teachers, so involve teachers carefully, but fully. Use core teachers, elective teachers, and school staff in the selection and development process to enhance communication and articulation of expectations. Parent-teacher organizations serve as outstanding groups to solicit parent involvement. This will, in turn, enhance the community's understanding of teaming. Confusion and lack of support are generated in communities where parents are not brought along with educators about key components in our school systems. Involving parents has real importance. As research has shown, there is a definite correlation between student achievement and parental involvement. Teaming needs the support and understanding of district constituency if it is truly to be effective.

145

While involvement is necessary, even more important is the provision for providing feedback to groups. Once plans begin taking shape status updates about teaming should be provided to help people understand how development is progressing. Involvement is communication with groups as well as committee work.

Build a Common Knowledge Base

Build a common base of knowledge for all participants. When teachers discuss teaming they need to have a common understanding of terminology and ideas. "There is, currently, a considerable amount of misunderstanding and confusion about the meaning of terms used to describe the organization for instruction in middle schools" (Alexander & George, 1981, p. 15). This misunderstanding will be prevalent as long as we have people attending different training institutions, seminars, workshops and conferences. The key for each district is to establish its own glossary so that everyone is working from the same frame of reference. Allow people to discuss and determine common references. Teachers will have a greater understanding if they are allowed to participate, so provide them the opportunity to be directly involved .

Train and Support Teams

Teams should have extensive inservice about expectations. Bring in current literature, current experts in teaming, and analyze and discuss the information with teachers. Make sure everyone understands not only aspects of teaming, but the rationale for utilizing these concepts. Teachers need to be able to see a need for teaming for it to be successful. Core teams are critical in the team development process because they not only help with initiating teaming and planning, they continue to provide feedback for success.

Begin with development of cadres in each building to facilitate teaming. Make them aware of current research and base line data regarding teaming concepts. Allow teams the opportunity in this process to decide their direction and the appropriateness of overall expectations. Have each team build an implementation plan. Recognize staff efforts as they progress through teaming. Recognition and awards come in a variety of ways. Sending people to national and state conferences, providing individuals with release time, or writing personal notes of appreciation are just a few methods. Know what your teachers consider as recognition and fill this need.

Critical to understanding teaming is the development of clear expectations which clarify its functions.

Confusion and lack of support are generated in communities where parents are not brought along with educators about key components in our school systems.

146

Figure 1

Teaming Expectations Guide								
						I - Introduce Concept	D - Develop Concept	M - Master Concept

Year One (six weeks)						Year		Expectations
1	2	3	4	5	6	2	3	The Team will:
I/D	M	M	M	M	M	M	M	Coordinate testing dates
I/D	M	M	M	M	M	M	M	Coordinate homework amounts per evening
I/D	M	M	M	M	M	M	M	Coordinate major project due dates
I	D	M	M	M	M	M	M	Establish a regular schedule of meetings
I	D	D	D	M	M	M	M	Coordinate parent conferencing
I	D	D	D	D	M	M	M	Conduct meetings that are: 1) structured 2) purposeful 3) productive
I	D	D	D	D	D	M	M	Know each other
I	D	D	D	D	D	D/M	M	Agree upon incentives, rules, consequences
I	D	D	D	D	D	D/M	M	Identify roles of team members
I	D	D	D	D	D	D/M	M	Understand the advantages and disadvantages of teaming
I	D	D	D	D	D	D	M	Have members that get along
	I	D	D	D	D	D/M	M	Share information regarding needs of students
	I	D	D	D	D	D/M	M	Plan activities for professional growth
			I	D	D	D/M	M	Share and discuss teaching strategies
			I	D	D	D	M	Correlate instructional objectives
			I	D	D	D	M	Plan one or two interdisciplinary units
			I	D	D	D	M	Group students for specific purposes
						I/D	M	Bring students together for occasional activities
						I/D	M	Establish team goals
							I/D/M	Visit students in other classes
							I/D/M	Coordinate cooperative field trips

Note: Any item may begin before the date suggested if a team is ready to progress. Any item not mastered by the date suggested should be reviewed and alternatives determined to accomplish the task.

Monitor Implementation

Another critical factor in the development of teams is evaluation. Too often this is one of the major overlooked areas. Conduct a pre-assessment, including questionnaires with community, staff, and students to discover each group's expectation. If a school is going to the effort to develop teaming, the school has a responsibility professionally to find out if teaming is meeting the expectations set forth. Listen carefully to people's opinion about teaming, to determine perceptions which need to be addressed further.

Conclusion

The major components of pre-planning include setting expectations, maximizing ownership, building a common knowledge base, training and support, and monitoring implementation. Concentration on these components will establish the skeletal structure to ensure effective teaming development within a similar environment. The framework described develops a common focus, common understanding, and common commitment to teaming. ▲

References

Alexander, W.M., & George, P.S. (1981). *The exemplary middle school.* NY: Holt, Rinehart, and Winston.

Merenbloom, E.Y. (1988). *The team process in the middle school: A handbook for teachers.* Columbus, OH: National Middle School Association.

Pickler, G. (1987). The evolutionary development of interdisciplinary teams. *Middle School Journal, 18*(2), 6-7.

Teaming:

The Heart of the Middle School

I. **Forming**
   Defining and Operationalizing

II. **Storming** (the prerequisite to norming)
   Once off the drawing board, what all teams experience.

III. **Norming**
   Rituals, Rights and Responsibilities

IV. **Transforming ... or reforming**
   Assessment and Evaluation

— Developed by Marion Payne,
Owen Brown Middle School

Evaluating Teams: Something to Grow On

Donna L. Rehbeck

To assess the success of teams and have them set goals, the author developed a flexible instrument for taking stock.

Because a formal evaluation could be used to eliminate programs, some educators shy away from engaging in this basic aspect of education. The utility of such an evaluation can be enhanced if teachers: 1) participate in developing the instrument; 2) review the results; 3) formulate plans to deal with problem areas identified; and 4) have the autonomy to implement the needed changes.

The interdisciplinary team lends itself to enhancing the evaluation process. As a vital component of middle school education, the teaching team can provide students with a program of support and individual attention while assisting those students in assimilating academic skills, developing social skills, understanding their emotional and physical growth, and exploring their interests. In addition, team members are viewed as parts of a professional support group that calls upon its members to work cooperatively towards self actualization so that they can serve their students effectively. Without a process of evaluation, it's not known if the teaching team is carrying out its many purposes.

Evaluating the functioning of a teaching team (as opposed to evaluating individual classroom teaching performance) can aid an administrator in staffing, identify for the staff areas that need attention (attitudes, parent involvement, etc.), assist in planning for the next semester or year, and improve the school program in general.

The procedures suggested and the instrument developed and described were aimed at improving the evaluation process and at evaluating the teaching team for the purposes mentioned.

The Evaluation Instrument

The early steps in developing the instrument include: 1) deciding who will evaluate; 2) deciding which factors are to be evaluated; and 3) determining how the data will be recorded and collected. Those people who have something at stake, those who share the responsibility for the students' growth and education, should be involved. While teachers are primarily involved in all aspects that could be considered for monitoring, input in formulating the evaluative instrument should also be sought for the administrative staff, parents, and students.

In evaluating the operation of the team itself, teachers need to look at factors that contribute to a successful teaming experience. As a team, teachers can devote a team meeting

149

to discussing the items that could be evaluated. Four areas are critical in team functioning: 1) the actions of the team leader; 2) the actions of the individual team members; 3) the actions of the team as a unit; and 4) the accomplishment of goals set by the teaching team. Each of the four areas can be broken down into an inventory of items to be evaluated.

The Team Leader. Whether the team leader is selected by team members or by the administration, leadership and the ability to manage can be appraised. Team members can articulate attributes that are important in a leader—particularly those attributes that deal with communication (notification and facilitation of meetings, words of commendation, etc.). The characteristics of a leader that contribute to the quality of person's work life such as maintaining an atmosphere that is open and being free from prejudice, should also be considered. Generally anything that a team leader does that affects the functioning of the team should be examined.

The Team Member. Literature concerning effective teaming stresses communication and shared responsibility as components needed for success. The team member has a responsibility to express differing views and ideas so that the best plans can be developed for the students' benefit. On an interdisciplinary team, team members are considered experts in particular content areas and are expected to share their knowledge. Behaviors such as attendance and record keeping, while not an accurate measure of a member's competence, may be included.

The sample survey included (p. 152) is intended for self appraisal. It is possible, however, that some teams may choose to have members evaluate one another. Depending upon the openness, involvement, and agreement of other role groups (counselors, parents, etc.), separate lists of items may be developed for those groups.

The Team Unit. After looking at team members and the team leader as individuals, the team's behavior as a unit should be examined. The goals outlined by the team at the beginning of the year and the responsibilities of any team at the middle level in regards to their students' intellectual, social, physical, and emotional growth will provide the items necessary to evaluate. Additional items to look at in this area may include parent/community communication and involvement, team support, and relationship of the team with the total school staff.

Without a process of evaluation, it's not known if the teaching team is carrying out its many purposes.

Individual Goal Areas. Using the goal statements developed by the team at the beginning of the year, team members can devise statements based on tasks to assess the attainment of those goals, especially those dealing with student accomplishment. Student self concept, development of responsibility for themselves, interpersonal relationships, and participation in school or community activities are areas that can be rated. Curriculum units, parent/community participation activities, exploratory opportunities, individual professional development (teacher) are also areas that can be assessed.

The sample included deals with student development of responsibility, things that students need to be responsible for such as homework, supplies, and deadlines.

Format

Once the areas to evaluate have been broken down into specific items, a format needs to be developed. The survey seems to be appropriate for the team's purposes. It can be completed anonymously, the responses can be easily tabulated, and problem areas can be quickly identified. The items identified that relate to the areas mentioned above need to be translated into statements that can be responded to and rated. The statements should also be phrased with the intended respondent in mind.

Team members may take the responsibility for developing statements for the specific areas. Some items might be combined and some eliminated. Keep the survey concise and short. If it is necessary to keep so many items that the survey will be lengthy, consider administering it in sections.

Procedures

After the instrument has been developed those groups who have something at stake in the results (administrators, teachers, students, and parents) should have an opportunity to review the statements for readability, appropriateness, and impartiality. Representatives from such organizations as the Student Council and the P.T.A. may be asked to read and react.

After the survey instrument has been prepared, times for its administration need to be determined. Teachers might respond during planning time. Students might respond during a planned group guidance period or be asked to respond at home and return the survey the following day. Parents may respond to the survey during a P.T.A. meeting or complete it at home and return it via their child. The team may decide that only a sampling from some groups is needed.

TEAM LEADER EVALUATION

Please complete this section by filling in the appropriate space on the right in response to the statements below.

	ALWAYS	FREQUENTLY	OCCASIONALLY	SELDOM	NEVER
1. My team leader makes it easy to discuss my concerns.					
2. My team leader seeks my opinions in planning.					
3. My team leader gave me adequate notice of team meetings.					
4. My team leader informed me prior to meetings about their content.					
5. My team leader conducted team meetings on time.					
6. My team leader conducted meetings with impartiality in discussions of a controversial nature.					
7. My team leader is effective in implementing team decisions.					
8. My team leader communicated team decisions, opinions, etc., to the administrative team.					
9. My team leader sought my opinion concerning student issues during the team meeting.					
10. My team leader told me when I did a good job.					
11. My team leader told me when I needed to reassess an action.					
12. My team leader did not discriminate against me because of age, race, sex, religion, or lifestyle.					

Likewise, an instrument to evaluate the effectiveness of the team as a unit could include items such as the following:

1. Student activities were planned that involved all students without the threat of competition.
2. Social activities were planned to provide students with the opportunity to interact with their peers. Decisions made by the team kept the needs of the students, rather than convenience, in mind. Parents were kept informed of student behavior, positive as well as negative.
5. Parents were invited to join school activities.
6. Parents were informed of student academic achievement, positive and negative.
7. Team members supported each other and were cooperative.
8. Responsibilities were shared on the team.
9. Curriculum planning occurred as a team.
10. Decision making was shared by the team
11. Students were involved in team planning and decision making.
12. Team members acknowledged accomplishments and shortcomings.

Using a similar format, the team member evaluation could include such items as the following:

1. I voiced my opinions on issues.
2. I accepted the different philosophies and opinions of my teammates and attempted to work with them.
3. I shared ideas with my team.
4. I willingly volunteered to accept responsibility for a team project.
5. I completed all record keeping on time.
6. I shared teaching strategies with my team.
7. I shared materials with my team.
8. I kept team problems within the team and did not discuss them with others.
9. I attended team meetings regularly; or, when absent, I sought out the content of the missed meeting.

The responsibility for data collection and recording can be shared by members of the teaching team. If computers are available, the recording can be simplified. Students may assist in recording data.

An examination of the collected data is necessary if positive changes are to result from the survey. Problem areas need to be identified, possible reasons for their existence discussed, and possible solutions proposed. If, for example, the survey indicates a lack of student involvement in planning activities, the team may then develop a structure that will include more students in planning.

The follow-up planning to improve the staff and program is crucial to the evaluation process.

All groups that directly affect the education of students should be involved in evaluation.

It may also be of interest to note discrepancies in data among respondents. Incongruity on the team may be noted by a high frequency of "SELDOM" or "NEVER" responses on the Team Evaluation, Team Leader Evaluation and/or the Team Member Evaluation. The special skills of an administrator may be required to work out a solution.

Follow-up

While the recording of survey data may be seen by some as the end result, the follow-up planning to improve the staff and program is crucial to the evaluation process. Plans should be carefully designed by those persons responding to the respective parts of the survey. Some plans may be as simple as devising a note to remind team members of a meeting.

On the other hand, an issue such as the degree of openness which is critical for allowing team members to express opinions may require some staff development that is concerned with group dynamics or the assistance of a school counselor.

Any growth which results from the follow-up could be noted from additional evaluation surveys.

Conclusion

For the evaluation process to be successful, all groups who directly affect the education of students should be involved in formulating the instrument as well as responding to it. The successful evaluation also depends upon the amount of attention focused on changing problems into progress. Such change can't occur unless teachers have the autonomy to implement needed changes with the support of the administration.

Changes in the instrument itself should be ongoing. Developing and conducting an evaluation program may take several years to refine. Each school and each team will have different items to rate, and the nature of each interest group (students, parents, administrators, etc.) will differ enough to call for variations on procedures.

The sample instrument could be a beginning. It looks primarily at the team staff. Additional evaluative factors can and should be developed for parent, student, and administrative involvement.

Evaluation requires that people and programs be exposed for examination. The conclusion drawn from the data collected should not be looked upon as reason for punishment or self reproach, but rather as something to grow on. ▲

> **All groups who directly affect the education of students should be involved in its development.**

Interdisciplinary Instruction: A Voyage Not a Harbor

JOHN H. LOUNSBURY

A candid look at the limitations of interdisciplinary instruction and some of the problems associated with its implementation.

In a volume specifically designed to promote interdisciplinary instruction, it may seem odd for the editor to close with a piece pointing out the weaknesses and limitations of this approach — but that is my intention.

Certainly I am not speaking against what this publication is encouraging, far from it. The merits of teaming are obvious, and they have been well delineated in these pages. Unfortunately, interdisciplinary teaming is still a minority practice in middle level schools, and that has to change. But along with my advocacy, I feel compelled to identify some problems that experience with teaming to date has made evident and to point out a factor that limits interdisciplinary teaming's potential. My fear is that, in its simplest and earliest form, teaming will become "institutionalized" and come to be viewed as our destination, the harbor, without recognition of its limitations or even its largest possibilities.

There is a fundamental limitation of interdisciplinary teaming that is inherent in the term itself. The label, when you stop to think about it, reflects an assumption that "disciplines" will continue to exist as entities, although they will now be related and occasionally even merged. The underlying assumption of the continuing existence of the subjects as such is undoubtedly one reason why fully integrated instruction has so seldom occurred. A teacher still sees herself as a science teacher or a social studies teacher even though now assigned to a team. And when not engaged in the occasional IDU, instruction is carried on in the usual departmentalized fashion. Although a number of major departures from discipline-based instruction are ongoing in middle schools around the country, these projects continue to be notable exceptions. Included in this volume are examples of both the more commonly found interdisciplinary units that are essentially correlations and the bolder problem-centered approaches. (for the latter see the articles, "Watershed: At the Confluence of Curricula," p. 131, and "Learning By Solving Real Problems," p. 123)

Putting aside the limitation inherent in the term, several problems with teaming have emerged. These can and should be alleviated to the extent possible. Doing so is not easy as has been demonstrated in the last two decades, but they must be openly recognized and attacked.

One problem is that while teaming has succeeded in reducing the personal isolation traditionally associated with departmentalized teaching, it has carried with it a loss in interteam interaction and a loss of identify with one's subject colleagues. Teachers, and often students, bemoan the lack of contact with those outside the team. Aware of this, faculties can make some arrangements to provide joint team activities and occasional opportunities for teachers of the various subjects to meet together, although maintaining departments as such is likely to inhibit the integrated approach needed.

An unfortunate dichotomy is set up between teams and exploratory faculty.

Another problem that is created when teams are organized is certainly unintentional, but no less real. An unfortunate dichotomy is set up between the teams and the exploratory teachers who instruct the team's students while the team members have common planning time. Often those unified arts and other so-called non-academic teachers come to feel like second-class citizens when the teams become the focus of activities and take on something of a special status. Since having common planning time is essential to effective teaming, this separation of a faculty into academic teams and others is rather inevitable. Its negative effects can be alleviated by efforts on the part of the academic teams to maintain regular communication and counter the division. Identifying a liaison person, sharing team minutes, and occasionally teaching for one of the exploratory teachers so that teacher can participate in the academic team's common planning time are among things that can be done.

Teaming has done little to address the teacher load problem.

Many schools organize their exploratory teachers into a team and schedule common planning time for them. (In some schools the academic teams are called *core teams* and the exploratory teams are called *encore teams*.) Other schools assign each of the specialist teachers to an academic team even though that teacher can't meet with the team during the school day — but can meet occasionally before or after school. Teachers who are on teams have an improved sense of efficacy and a better image of themselves as professionals than do those not on teams. Therefore, efforts should be made to extend the benefits of teaming to all faculty.

The division of a faculty into academic teams and exploratory teachers also makes it difficult to integrate the arts into meaningful learning experiences. Having unified arts faculty easily accessible as resource persons would be a boon to all parties. Flexibility and imaginative scheduling can open doors that will permit areas and faculty outside the "big four" to play a genuine role in the academic program.

One of the major problems with interdisciplinary teaming, in my judgment, is that it has done relatively little to address the long-standing teacher load problem. When a team is composed of four or five teachers, as most are, the number of different students each teacher comes in contact with daily exceeds one hundred, sometimes even 130 or more. The personal influence that middle school teachers could have and should have is limited by a single 45-50 minute period a day as their only contact with a student. A teacher who spends just 50 minutes a day with 120+ different youngsters cannot know them and influence them as well as a teacher who spends 100 minutes a day with just 60 different youngsters — half as many students and twice as long with them. In the typical seven period day teachers find themselves so busy teaching "classes" that they don't have time to direct the education of youth.

Fortunately, there is beginning to emerge a trend to reduce the size of teams, especially at the sixth grade level where there really is no need for four or five separate subject specialists and where there still exists a need for a "mother hen" or two. The personal-social needs of young adolescents are such that they thrive best in a deeper relationship with a caring professional than can be established in a single period a day where the individual is always just one of 30 or more students that are treated as a group. It is easier to establish a true learning community with 60 students than with 120 students.

As interdisciplinary teaming has played out in classrooms across the country an already existing and, in my judgment, serious weakness in most classroom instruction is still present. It is in no way caused by teaming. In fact, it is less prevalent with teaming but it is still too frequently found. The passivity of learning still characterizes most middle level schools and has been documented many times in national studies. It is a handicap to effective learning and personal development. Students are usually cast as passive recipients of teachers' judgments about what they should learn and what activities they should engage in. Although interdisciplinary teaming has provided a marvelous opportunity to involve students in helping to decide both what to study and how best to learn it, typically it has not been exploited sufficiently.

Teachers in common planning time or sometimes in summer workshops develop a unit fully, selecting activities each can use to achieve the objectives agreed on which relate to a particular subject's curriculum. The result is that all too often an interdisciplinary unit only teaches better what probably shouldn't be taught in the first place and leaves students as the passive consumers of others' decisions, much as they were in departmentalized instruction. The planning done by teachers apart from students should be to develop a *resource* unit not a *teaching* unit. Drawing on various options and an abundance of ideas in a resource unit, the teacher and students together should fashion the actual teaching unit. Ownership results from active

> Teachers are so busy teaching "classes" that they don't have time to direct the education of youth.

> The ultimate goal of integrated instruction goes far beyond correlation and fusion.

157

involvement, and active involvement leads to the kind of learning that alters behavior.

It needs to be acknowledged as well that just because some cross-subject connections can be made they should not be pursued unless such activities specifically serve valid objectives. Artificially creating correlations just for the sake of having them is not educationally productive or proper. Better to merge just two subjects rather than forcing the unnatural involvement of all four basic subjects.

It is also important to recognize that the fundamental reform called for today requires a major change in the school's culture and climate, not just in one organizational feature.Changes in a school's ethos are not automatic by-products of the administrative organization of teams. However, the climate in which teaming tends to exist is usually positive and may be as important to integrated instruction as the teaming itself. A supportive and positive climate must be pervasive and conducive to all efforts and means of achieving a developmentally appropriate curriculum for 10-14 year olds. Putting too much hope for reform and curriculum change in merely organizing teams is a mistake.

Clearly, the ultimate goal of fully integrated instruction goes far beyond correlating and even beyond the fusing of two or more subjects. It leads to problem-solving in which any area of knowledge that can contribute to the solution of the problem at hand can be called on in the manner of the true core curriculum. The curriculum in such cases is the result of student-teacher planning without any content "givens." Teams in middle schools of the future will not likely be composed of representatives from the "big four," but rather be representative of a diversity of talents, interests, and backgrounds.

The creation of interdisciplinary teams, then, is the right step to take for most middle level schools, but not the only or final step. Needed opportunities for integrating instruction and improving learning for kids are created immediately by teaming. Yet the full benefits of teaming come slowly and even have their limits. Establishing teams is only a stop-over on the never ending voyage to achieve truly life-like integrated instruction, not a harbor in which to rest. ▲

> **Too often an IDU just teaches better what shouldn't be taught in the first place.**

For Further Information

Listed here are key articles and monographs plus sources of actual units.

Arhar, Joanne, (Ed.) (1992, Spring). *Research in Middle Level Education, Vol 15,* No. 2. Columbus, OH: National Middle School Association. 82 pages, $12.00.

Five research studies selected from many submissions plus a thoughtful introductory essay by the editor all dealing with teaming comprise this theme issue of NMSA's research publication. Each study is presented thoroughly in this valuable new resource.

Beane, James A. (1989). *A Middle School Curriculum: From Rhetoric to Reality.* Columbus, OH: National Middle School Association. 84 pages, $9.00.

A truly important, "breakthrough" publication that has done much to advance current efforts to improve the curriculum itself. Should be read — and contemplated — by all serious middle level educators. Includes both a reasoned rationale and a proposal.

Brodhagen, B., Weilbecker, G., and Beane, J. (1992, June). "Living in the Future: An Experiment with an Integrative Curriculum." *Dissemination Services in the Middle Grades,* ELI, P.O. Box 863, Springfield, MA.

A description of an experiment in integrated curriculum after the manner suggested by Beane. Carried out successfully in a culturally diverse eighth grade that included ED and LD students by a team that truly practices student-teacher planning. Informative and inspiring.

Selected Resources on Interdisciplinary Instruction

Erb, Thomas and Doda, Nancy (1989). *Team Organization: Promise — Practices and Possibilities.* Washington, DC: National Education Association.128 pages.

A well-prepared, functional and comprehensive treatise on teaming. Covers most all pertinent topics including a chapter on teaching with interdisciplinary units. Written with the teacher in mind.

Dickinson, Thomas (Ed.) (1992). *Readings in Middle Level Curriculum: A Continuing Conversation.* Columbus, OH: National Middle School Association. (in press)

A re-publication of significant curriculum articles that have appeared in the *Middle School Journal,* these twenty-one articles (two new ones included) provide the best collection of serious and contemporary thinking on the middle school curriculum issue available anywhere.

Integrating the Curriculum (October, 1991). *Educational Leadership,* Association for Supervision and Curriculum Development, Alexandria, VA.

This theme issue of ASCD's journal contains an extensive collection of articles that deal directly or indirectly with interdisciplinary instruction. Among the many authors included are Vars, Beane, Jacobs, Brophy, Hurd, and Fogarty. A valuable source of ideas and information.

Jacobs, Heidi (Ed.) (1989). *Interdisciplinary Curriculum: Design and Implementation.* Alexandria, VA: Association for Supervision and Curriculum Development. 95 pages, $13.95.

This volume is widely recognized as a good source on interdisciplinary teaching. Although it is not restricted to the middle level it is most apropos. The Interdisciplinary Concept Model (ICM) for planning a unit is detailed by the author/editor.

Jenkins, John M. and Tanner, Daniel (Eds.) (1992). *Restructuring for an Interdisciplinary Curriculum.* Reston, VA: National Association of Secondary School Principals. 110 pages.

This new volume provides much food for thought. Although directed more to the high school than the middle school, a chapter on a three-period, single teacher core program in a California middle school is a highlight. An excellent historical chapter opens the volume.